This book is dedicated to the riders,
old and new. May we all ride safe
and have a lot of fun riding it.

The Adventures You'll Have Riding Motorcycles

The world of Cruisers, Sportbikes, Dirtbikes & everywhere they can take you

By Lee ' RideFar' Heaver

This book is sold with the understanding that neither the author nor the publisher is hereby rendering legal advice. If such advice is required, the personal services of a competent professional legal counsel should be sought.

Motorcycles are dangerous. Your mother told you so. Riding a motorcycle exposes you to increased risks of all kinds. You can get seriously hurt or worse. Ride with caution, take lots of training, and wear your motorcycle gear. This book should not be the only thing you read when learning to ride motorcycles. Motorcycle riding requires real world training.

Cataloguing in Publication data available from Library and Archives Canada

ISBN [978-1-9990572-0-6] (print)
ISBN [978-1-9990572-1-3] (ebook)
ISBN [978-1-9990572-2-0] (audiobook)
This is an original digital edition of *The Adventures You'll Have Riding Motorcycles*

Your Table of Contents

Make notes and page numbers here for stuff you want to reference

INTRODUCTION

The next chapter of your life is about to begin. Welcome to the thrilling and fulfilling life of motorcycle riding. Given that motorcycles can ride almost anywhere, you have options.

Lots of options. That's why I wrote this book. You have so much to choose from. Where do you begin? Treat this book as a "choose your own adventure." Pick the chapters that speak to you. Most motorcyclists don't do everything, and you don't have to either. As you ride motorcycles, your riding will evolve. So you can always come back to this book and read what you missed. If you do read the whole book, you'll have enough information to get started. The chapters are set up to get you excited.

If you're new to riding, you've entered a new stage of your life. How do you get the most out of riding a motorcycle? You might feel overwhelmed by all the choices and rides you can go on. You might also worry about riding on your own – but do you really have to? Riding a motorcycle can be anything you want it to be. It can be your thing, a great social activity with new friends, or a way of life (like me!). One of the best things you can do is just ride. You have the skills, so use them. You'll be amazed how rusty you will feel after not riding for a while. If you've just taken a motorcycle course, they usually include road rides or offer them for a small fee. I highly recommend these. An instructor will lead you around the area you learned in. Think of it as a guided tour of your community3. With the added safety of the instructor leading and the company of fellow students, this is a great introduction to riding on the street. If you have your own motorcycle, you can bring it on the road ride. What better way to get used to the road than by riding your own motorcycle? Be sure to try and lead a few rides if possible, as following riders all the time makes it harder to feel confident on your own. If you are riding with other newer riders, ask for their contact details so you can ride and learn together.

If you already know how to ride and you're getting back into it, taking a refresher course, a private lesson, or even an advanced course will quickly get you back on two wheels. Our bodies and minds never forget how to ride motorcycles. You just need an hour or two to get the skills back. You'll be better than you think.

It can be intimidating out there, and if you are still hesitant about riding on your own, go during the quieter times. Early mornings, midday, and evenings can be great times to ride. Avoid rush hour. Less traffic means less for you to focus on, so you can relax more and get used to riding on the street. Feeling comfortable is good, but you should be going for confident. Don't overdo it, as things can change fast. You may not have the skills to react quickly and correctly in a surprise situation. Be slow and smooth; abrupt reactions can cause problems where there were no problems before.

Staying closer to home also offers extra confidence. You'll never be far from home if you make a mistake. Ultimately, just remember to take those deep breaths and keep a wide focus – don't keep your eyes glued narrowly on what's ahead of you. Make sure you relax, lose the death grip on your controls, and don't cover your controls.

As you ride along the roads, you must go the speed limit. If this is too fast for you, stay on the quiet roads for the start of your ride. It is dangerous to be the slowest-moving vehicle on the road. The confidence at the speed limit will come quickly. Once you get the hang of riding at the speed limit and moving with the flow of traffic, you will quickly become comfortable, and going too slow will be a thing of the past. Before you know it, your problem will be quite the opposite.

Going with the flow of traffic is the safest way to ride. Some riders like to go a little faster so nothing sneaks up on them, but this can be problematic, as you don't want to be breaking speeding laws and increasing the risk to yourself. Go with the flow. Lane positioning can be equally important. Always be in the dominant lane position. Most of the time it is the left-hand side of the lane, but in some cases it is the right-hand side of the lane. It really depends on traffic and even the country you ride in.

If you find yourself riding faster than everyone else on the road, you will increase your odds of crashing, and you'll have plenty of fines and penalties coming your way. Part of the thrill of riding a motorcycle comes from that rush of speed, but keep it in check. If you can't, motorcycling might be an interest you learn to regret. Excessive speed has its place, and it is not on city streets.

I am sure it has dawned on you that you are riding nothing more than an engine with two wheels strapped on. This is a great part of the experience, but you are exposed. Show discipline and even if you are on a smaller motorcycle (300cc or less), remember that it is still faster than most vehicles on the road. Your bike will not try to hurt you, but your mistakes will. Motorcycles are built incredibly well these days, so it really is up to you. Be smooth on the controls and your motorcycle can be very safe.

If you are looking for extra confidence on the road, motorcycle gear is your ticket. Consider it a requirement for riding. What may seem like a small amount of protection is actually quite a bit. If you are feeling restricted by the bulk and tightness of the gear, I promise you will get used to it. It really is amazing stuff and will give you great odds for making it through a crash with little to no injury. Do not leave home without it.

If you managed to keep in contact with your fellow students from your motorcycle course, ride with them. If you are self-taught, find them on social groups such as Facebook or online forums in your city. I've found the best way to keep in touch with riders is a group chat in WhatsApp, Facebook Messenger, etc. Most people are reluctant to start one, so you might need to take some initiative. Once you have a small number of riders, it will grow fast. New riders never have enough people to ride with. You'll soon learn of the new rider hangouts, and those are the places to be on sunny days.

Once you find the motorcycling social scene, don't be shy. The fact that you are a new rider is not an issue. Even if you find difficulty in talking to new people, it is a lot easier with a motorcycle because you will already have something in common. Riders are naturally social. All you have to do is start chatting bikes. Ask what others are riding. Just give someone a chance to talk about their motorcycle and you'll have a new rider friend. This is also a great chance to talk about the good local roads – they may even tell you about the secret ones.

Before you know it, you will have a new social circle of friends, and people who start out as your new motorcycle friends may soon become your motorcycle family. You'll be riding together and creating memories and camaraderie for many days to come. This is the social nature of motorcycling. If this all sounds like too much, there are plenty of solo riders out there, too.

Motorcycling can be whatever you want it to be. This book is here to show you all the possibilities it can bring you. I started riding in 2005, and it has completely shaped my life. I look back on the moment I decided to start riding and wonder just how different my life would be if I hadn't. It's a safe bet it wouldn't be this interesting and exciting. So where will you go?

Chapter ONE

Your First Rides

You've learned to ride and now comes the regular riding part. Maybe you're getting back into riding. As you just read, your initial (or return to) riding is very important. This is where you build the comfort and confidence. What were considered big rides are now small rides as you want to go farther and farther on your motorcycle. Going on bigger rides is like running in a marathon: you have to work up to it.

Gaining confidence

No one learns at the same speed and pace. The course I teach is an excellent fit for most, but still, everyone learns at their own pace. If I have students that need more time, no problem. We all get there eventually. It is very important that you not be hard on yourself if it is taking longer to gain the confidence you desire. Take as long as you need and be patient. Rushing it can lead to painful mistakes. If at any time you feel tired or scared, take a break. Most motorcycle rides are all about going for coffee, so enjoy that cinnamon scone with extra butter at the closest coffee shop. Like meditation, motorcycle breaks give you a mental reset, so you're better prepared for the rest of your ride. Take those breaks, so you can do those bigger rides you desire.

While it may be comforting to do the same ride over and over, you can become complacent with the route. Vary your rides so you are always in the prepared mindset and so you are always dealing with different situations like lane positioning and spacing. This is also a good time to find that empty parking lot and practice emergency maneuvers. No doubt you learned them in a course, and now it's time to practice them on the motorcycle you own. All motorcycles stop and move differently. You have to understand and be comfortable with doing the emergency maneuvers on your motorcycle. This includes emergency stops in a straight line and even on a corner. It is also a good idea to practice quick and smooth swerving.

If I could get every rider to practice these exercises on their new bike with their new skills, I am sure it would reduce accidents with new riders. Really understand and build that confidence on your motorcycle.

Figure eights. These are endless U-turns in both directions. If you were to track the movement of your tires, it would make the number eight on the pavement. Start with a big figure eight then make it as tight as you can handle. Consistent speed is key. Steady on the throttle. Keep the clutch in the friction zone.

Emergency stops in a straight line. Get up to speed (the higher the better) and stop that motorcycle as quickly as you can without your automatic braking system (ABS). If your motorcycle does have ABS, stomp on the rear brake until it engages. Know what it feels like.

Emergency stops on a corner. You should know that braking on a corner is a very bad idea. The key here is to straighten up and then apply the brakes. While this does not leave a lot of room in a corner, it is quite possible to slow down significantly when you take the right line into the corner. Mid-corner, straighten the motorcycle and then apply the brakes smoothly and progressively.

Quick starts. We always run the risk of getting rear-ended. So always be ready to go when you're stopped. A quick start requires very smooth clutch use. If we are surprised, our chances of stalling are quite high. Practice those quick getaways.

When you first start, please be especially careful around intersections. My local insurance company tells me that 73 per cent of their claims come from intersections. There is nothing wrong with slowing slightly and having a second look before you continue through. Please do not keep your eyes forward and power through the intersection. That places far too much trust in the traffic around you. You'll find more safety on highways, as the flow of traffic is constant. Yes, speeds are higher, but stats still show that highways are safer.

You'll be able to venture out farther and farther as your confidence builds. You'll be eager to get on the highway, as the higher speed feels more stable on the motorcycle. If the speed still scares you, take your time. You don't need to rush to riding on the highway. Once you start to ride on the highways, you'll soon come to enjoy them. There is a lot less going on. The higher speed is enjoyable, and you'll love the feeling of the cruise. Stats show the highways are safer places to ride, but the higher speeds can mean bigger crashes so keep focused. Complacency can be a rider's worst nightmare.

As you ride, keep your expectations low. This may sound strange but don't think you've figured it out all too quickly. Start with smaller rides and work your way up. Just like a marathon runner slowly increases their running distance, so should you. What may happen on a big ride is you have ventured quite far away and would like to stop riding. Being tired and staring down a big long ride home may put you at additional risk. Motorcycle riding is a physical and mental challenge. That is what makes it so rewarding. We crave the challenge, but we must respect our limits.

Practicing safety

It doesn't take long to gain comfort with riding, but are you ready for a surprise? Probably not. That's OK – most riders are not ready for a surprise. Things happen fast and as a new rider your reactions will not be ready. It is one thing to learn emergency maneuvers, but it is another thing to implement them when the moment comes. As mentioned before, it does take a lot of practice to make proper reactions automatic. We are naturally apt to do the wrong thing in critical moments. Be as relaxed as you can when you ride. Being on the edge or really nervous will force us to make the wrong decision. The brain has no good ideas when scared or nervous. This is why you cannot cut short the practice time that will make you ready for the emergency maneuvers. It's a bit of a catch-22: we do need to ride on the streets to build our comfort and confidence. This is where riding with others can be an excellent strategy.

Riding with other people provides a great sense of safety. Strength in numbers. In a riding group you can watch out for each other and point out any mistakes. This is where good social bonds can be built, too. Riding with others is a great experience, but you should ride individually as well. Riding in a group can allow us to be less vigilant. Riding solo means we must be more aware and careful. Be sure to balance your riding time. Some people never get the confidence of solo riding because they ride in groups all the time – myself included. Once I started riding in groups I was addicted to the social nature. It was just cool to be riding in a group, too. In restaurants and coffee shops we were always the group laughing and having the most fun. Then when I rode on my own it was so quiet. I felt more exposed, as I was not used to riding solo. As with most things, balance is key.

Being perseverant

Motorcycle riding is different for everyone. Every class I teach is a diverse group of people all with different reasons for getting into riding. That also means everyone learns at different speeds. I find 90 per cent of people I teach pick it up in the time I am teaching them. The other 10 per cent need another hour (or two) or another day to figure it out and pass our test. This is completely normal. Please don't be hard on yourself if it is taking more time to learn. I know this all too well. Not from motorcycling but from learning piano and surfing. After over a year of piano lessons, I could barely play my way through "Twinkle, Twinkle Little Star," and with surfing, I had to swallow gallons of sea water to get up and stay up on a surfboard. Grit and perseverance are key to learning anything. If you are feeling pessimistic about your ability to ride motorcycles, stay with it. This is where riding a bicycle in addition to your motorcycle will help. Anyone can ride motorcycles, including you.

Be patient and don't let frustration and aggression get the best of you. Keep at it. When you make a mistake don't kick your helmet down the lot and yell out a giant F-bomb. You'll scare children and small animals. Keep going and take some deep breaths. If you need a break, take it. Pull your helmet off, relax, slap yourself around a bit, and get back out there. If your stress levels get too high, try again tomorrow. If you are too stressed out, the cortisol rushing through your blood is not helping you learn. It short-circuits your brain and makes it hard to make those natural decisions to ride a motorcycle smoothly.

What happens if riding is not for you? Anyone can ride motorcycles but whether they should is another question. I will never tell a student they should not ride motorcycles, but I will educate them enough that they can make the decision on their own. The standout reason that you should not ride motorcycles is situational awareness. If you have poor situational awareness, you just are not aware of what is around you. I call those Bird Box riders: they should not ride a motorcycle. A quick test of whether you have good or bad situational awareness is how you cross intersections when walking. If you ever run out to cross the road without checking left and right or over your shoulder, you have poor situational awareness.

Other reasons include how hard you use the brakes. The front brake requires a very smooth and progressive hand when using it. Some riders use it like a light switch, off or on. The motorcycle does not like this, and your braking may very well cause you to crash. It can take time to slow your hands down. This doesn't go well if you are very intimidated by traffic. You must show confidence and never assume your space or the space you are moving into is clear. It is unnerving being the smallest vehicle on the road, but remember you can get yourself out of bad situations easier than other vehicles because of your small size.

If you never like riding in traffic, maybe the track or dirt riding is for you. Just doing track days on motorcycles is an option. This way you just get to ride with other riders on a race track. It is not a race. You do not need to be a racer (or have a race license) to enjoy the many great race tracks around us. Many riders choose to ride on the track only. Lastly, dirt biking may be what is for you. Out in the dirt roads and more adventurous roads, dirt bikes are quite at home. There is a greater risk of injury as all those rocks and trees can be tricky. Explore all options for riding a motorcycle. Not only is it fun, it'll make you a better rider.

Your first 1,000 kilometers or miles will be filled with fun, laughs, and the occasional scary moment. Enjoy it. Motorcycling does demand respect, especially on those first rides but you can do it. We are far more capable than we give ourselves credit for. Patience, perseverance, and grit is key to becoming confident (not just comfortable) riding motorcycles. So don't rush the process, enjoy it as you will make lasting memories being the newbie rider.

Chapter TWO

Basic Riding Techniques

At this point, you should know that your body is pretty important to how the motorcycle rides. Moving your arms and legs excessively (especially at low speeds) doesn't work. Be one with your motorcycle; be a statue on your motorcycle. Squeeze your knees into the bike and tighten up your core muscles. This is where good riding starts.

Good riding techniques are key to confidence. They also come from the laws of physics, so it is best to follow them. When you and your motorcycle operate as one, you'll start to get those moments of Zen. It is also why people have closer relationships with their motorcycles than with their cars.

The good news with basic riding techniques is that they require minimal effort and you don't need to be an athlete to do what is required. It does help to be at a good level of fitness and activity, as with anything. The more you ride, the more you will see that the average rider is not competing in the Olympics. This is good news and one of the many reasons riding is available to everyone.

Let's start with looking where you want to go. No doubt this advice has been yelled at you several times if you took a riding course. Expect to hear it for the rest of your riding life. I still heard it myself on my most recent advanced motorcycle rider course. Even the motorcyclists I interview say looking where they want to go is what benefited their riding the most. So no matter what, look where you want to go.

The faster you go, the more important looking where you want to go becomes. What happens here is time begins to slow down. If you focus directly in front of you or do not look far enough, everything moves by quickly. This is too much information for our brains to process. This is where mistakes can happen. The farther ahead we look, the slower things appear. This allows for easier decision making. The dilemma we face on the street (versus the track) is the surface condition. Gravel in a corner can really ruin our day or give us a moment of lost traction. So how do you balance this? By being reasonable and respectful of the speed you carry on the street. It is also wise to enter a corner slower. We never know what hazards a corner may have.

Now let's move your body over to the left or right. The simple act of moving your butt off the seat helps dramatically with cornering. This is a subtle movement: your butt will not be hanging off the seat. Just move one cheek. Cornering to the left? As you approach the corner, shift your butt to the left, so your left butt cheek is off the seat. That's it. It will feel awkward at first, but you will get used to it. By shifting your weight to the left, the motorcycle will want to corner to the left. The same is true with shifting your weight to the right. The benefits of this practice are highly worthwhile. With your weight to one side of the motorcycle, the centre of the motorcycle tire is being used more than the side of it. If you spend most of your time in the middle of the seat the tire has to do more work, which means you are using the sides of your tire. That's fine. It just means that you have less to corner with if you need it. The sides of the motorcycle tire do not have as much traction as the centre. This simple act of moving your butt off the seat gives you more traction from your tires. This is a huge benefit to your safety.

So when do we use our body for cornering? A simple answer is at any speed over 30 km/h (20 mph). At speeds lower than this, it is not beneficial. As you approach the corner, shift your body over, look where you want to go, and go for it. If you are riding a sport bike, you might feel the need to significantly lean off the motorcycle like MotoGP riders do. That is overdoing it. Keep it simple.

So what about all of our other body parts?

Your head is the highest point on the motorcycle. Given its size and weight, it does play a role in cornering. Look where you want to go and move your head forward towards the motorcycle. Move your head closer to the mirror. Some instructors have told me to try and lick or kiss the mirror. That's a good way to put it. That said, on straight roads lowering your head all the way to the gas tank makes you feel like a racer but doesn't do a lot for street riding. It's like a giant spoiler on a car – looks like you're racing but does nothing at speeds under 160 km/h (100 mph).

Your torso and chest should point in the direction you want to go because (you guessed it) they help you look where you want to go. It also helps with your arm positioning. Your arms should be somewhat relaxed and definitely not stiff. They need to absorb the imperfections of the road. Stiff arms will make you sore and possibly force errors on your part. Same goes with your hands: please have a loose grip on the bars and not a death grip. It is extremely difficult to operate your hands and arms while tense. You already know how sensitive the throttle is. A loose grip will give you a more steady, controlled hand.

Let's not forget about your legs and feet. You can stick your knee out or keep it against the motorcycle, whatever you are more comfortable with. Your feet should be planted firmly on the pegs. Pressing down lightly will lower the centre of gravity, which is a good thing. You can also push down the left foot peg, and this will push the motorcycle to the left subtly. Same goes with the right foot peg. This won't, however, work for Harley-Davidsons or any motorcycle with forward controls. You just can't push down on the pegs when your foot is forward. When you can, pushing your feet into the pegs is a great way to initiate corners, as it is the lowest centre of gravity.

The physics of motorcycle cornering are fascinating and challenging. I would much rather corner all day long than go for high-speed runs in a straight line. Your body positioning also depends on what motorcycle you ride. Cornering is the most technical and challenging on sport bikes, as they have the greatest cornering abilities. The foot pegs on sport bikes are higher up, which can lead to discomfort but also allow them to lean over farther. Cruisers cannot lean over too far because their floorboards will start to scrape. Dirt bikes won't scrape foot pegs, but their skinnier tires don't allow for extreme lean angles. With sport bikes and dirt bikes, moving your butt left and right with the corners works wonderfully. With cruisers, the shape of the seat really prevents this, so move your torso instead.

This chapter lightly touches on all the possibilities with body positioning. I strongly encourage you to work with instructors and other skilled riders to find the body positioning that works for you. It takes time, so be patient. Switching motorcycles also means relearning how to corner effectively. The more bikes you ride, the easier it will be to figure out the right amount of body positioning for all those great corners. The above explanations are also for smooth and clean roads. When we have excellent traction, leaning your body into the corner is a great idea. Once we start riding on a gravel surface, you do not want to lean off the bike. The loose surface doesn't work well with body positioning. Keep yourself in the centre of the seat. When we have traction from a smooth surface, body positioning matters.

What about dragging your knee or pulling giant wheelies?

I do get this question as I teach new riders. They want the excitement, I get it. It is a thrill and does give me a good idea that I am near the limits of my traction. If you really, really want to do it, dragging your knee should be done on a track or a safe, closed environment (empty parking lot). Keep in mind that it may slow you down. I see riders all the time stretching their knee out as much as possible to feel it scrape along the road. You want to bring the road to your knee and not your knee to the road. Use your proper body positioning and be smooth. The smoother you are the faster you will be. When my knee starts to scrape along the road, I know I am doing it right, as I am not trying to get it to the road surface.

Be patient with dragging a knee as it could lead to unnecessary and painful learning experiences. There are plenty of fast riders who never drag a knee. Everyone has their own technique to cornering. Dragging a knee can be fun and thrilling, but it is not required.

Next up is bringing that front tire off the ground. Riding motorcycles is challenging enough with two wheels on the ground, and just having one seems crazy. Please don't try to learn wheelies on your brand new motorcycle. That is a dangerous learning curve. If you really want to do this right, start with learning how to ride a unicycle. You will be balancing on one wheel. Next you can move to a BMX bike.

Most won't take this route. If that is you, seek out the training of a motorcycle stunter. Any reasonably large city has a stunting community. Find them and introduce yourself. They can be intimidating riders and the style of their stunting videos shows that. The local stunter in my city, Matt Bush, is one of the friendliest stunters I know. He loves it and wants to show everyone how fun it is. He does caution anyone wanting to learn to pull wheelies and stunt that you can seriously hurt yourself. If you can't miss work or family obligations due to a stunting accident, best you leave the wheelies to the professionals. There is a chapter on stunting in this book. Skip ahead if that's what you want to do.

Your motorcycle is your dance partner

You and your motorcycle are in this together. Your motorcycle is your dance partner. If you are a horrible dancer, I have good news: riding a motorcycle is a lot easier than learning to dance. What is common between the two is the gracefulness. You must move slowly and methodically with your motorcycle. It will do almost anything you tell it to do as long as you are slow about it. Moving your body should be done in slow motion. When things happen fast around you, move your body slow. This smooth weight transfer is excellent, and your motorcycle will reward you with a beautiful line through a corner.

Body positioning is a never-ending skill that needs practice. When I got my new motorcycle, I signed up for instruction. While the two motorcycles I was going between were not radically different, the instructor was able to offer a few observations that would help me corner the new-to-me motorcycle. I am sure I would have figured it out eventually (or maybe not) but having that instruction made it obvious. Every year I ride, I want some feedback on my body positioning, as I may get too lazy.

Chapter THREE

Good Riding Etiquette

Riding with others is an experience that makes motorcycling even more incredible. When we share a newfound passion with others, it heightens the fun for everyone. Had I not started riding with others, I don't think I would have kept riding motorcycles. I remember my first group rides. We would spend all morning riding and then stop for lunch. We overwhelmed every restaurant we stopped at. We were the liveliest bunch there. Conversation was fast and fun and by the time lunch was over, we were excited for the second half of our ride. At the end of the ride, we either waved goodbye and took our road home or stopped to high-five a great ride. By the time we got home, we were already planning the next ride.

When you ride with others, there is great safety in numbers. A motorcycle group commands attention and respect. Traffic on the road will give you the space and respect you rightly deserve. So let's go through the rules, both legal and common sense. If you are completely new to group riding, always introduce yourself. Most riders won't approach you first. You'll have to say hello. This will let everyone know you're new to the ride or group. This is a good thing. They'll be able to put you in the right spot and with the right riders. The leader of the group should know the route. Seems pretty obvious, but sometimes motorcyclists just ride with little other reason other than to just ride. If there is a plan, get as much information about the route as possible. Getting separated is no fun. If you feel comfortable with the riders, exchange cell phone numbers. Knowing each other's contact details maximizes the possibilities of coping with any incident, minor or major. Now you're ready to get going.

When you ride with others, there is great safety in numbers. A motorcycle group commands attention and respect. Traffic on the road will give you the space and respect you rightly deserve. So let's go through the rules, both legal and common sense.

At a stop sign or a red light, you will stop two by two. You're on the left side, and the next rider is right beside you. When it is your turn to go, both riders move off the line together, but you can no longer ride side by side. Unless you're a Hells Angel or a police officer, riding side by side is not permitted. It is also not safe. You have no escape route beside you. If you have to avoid a large object in your lane, your options are limited, as another rider is right beside you. What if you are riding alone and you come upon another solo rider? You can still pull up beside them, just not right beside them. Respect that they arrived first by stopping just before they did. If you stop right beside them, it might be a challenge (drag race?) or they might think you are going to pull ahead. Keep the nonverbal communication clear, and let them be ahead of you.

Riding in a staggered formation is key to riding safely with others. The lead rider picks a side of the road, left or right. If the lead rider picks the left side, the second rider will be on the right side and about one to two seconds behind them. The third rider will be on the left side and about one to two seconds behind the second rider. This repeats for every rider that is part of the group. If the rider ahead of you is on the left side, you will be on the right side, one to two seconds behind. Now you can move to the side if necessary or speed up or slow down without fear of coming too close to the other riders. This organized riding is highly visible to other traffic and safe for the riders. If you are riding solo and come upon another solo rider, staggered riding is required. The distance between the riders varies with speed. In city traffic, the space should be just enough that cars or trucks will not merge into your group. On highways, you will be more spread out, as the higher speed will leave you less time for reaction.

On one my big rides, the staggered riding formation saved a crash. We were riding through the Salt Flats of Utah. The air was crisp and clean, and it was super bright. The bright blue sky and ultra-white salt were tough on the eyes. All of a sudden, the lead rider slowed and was behind me before I had time to react. Had I been following directly behind them, I would have rear-ended them causing a crash. It turned out there was a speed trap up ahead. Slowing down for a speed trap is common, but that reaction was aggressive. Staggered riding formation kept this to just a mistake and not a crash.

So what do you do when riding through a corner? Everyone takes their own line. It will almost seem like you are riding in a single line. The real key here is where you are looking. Look far through the corner and not at the rider in front of you. If the rider ahead of you goes off the road, you will most likely follow them off the road. Look ahead of them so if they go off, you carry on. The best practice for cornering with other riders is to keep more space: the closer you are to the rider in front of you, the more you are exposed to their mistakes. This is especially true if you are riding with people you've never ridden with before.

Passing other motorcyclists and vehicles demands respect. Respect for the person you are passing. Motorcycles enjoy speed, so passing happens fast. Good for us, surprising for vehicles of any other size. Be mindful and predictable. Make sure the vehicle knows you're there and wanting to pass. Try to avoid passing too fast. Put yourself in the car or truck you're passing. You're cruising along the road at your pace and all of sudden a pack of motorcycles flies past you. It's surprising and may cause an unintended reaction. If your pass is safe, you can also add in a wave to the motorist. This may possibly diffuse any tensions down the road. Passing other motorcyclists is the same. As motorcyclists, we don't expect to be passed. It is very common for motorcyclists to initiate the pass without shoulder checking. There is a very, very low chance someone will be there. I get it. Some motorcyclists (even in the group you like so much) pass without enough warning. If you are going to pass another motorcycle, get their attention. Maybe even get a wave from them before passing.

The key to riding with groups is riding your own ride. Everyone has varying levels of skill and risk tolerance. What is comfortable for you may not be comfortable for them. Be respectful of the space because things change fast. Even better, have a riding buddy. Sometimes groups can be challenging to ride with. Having a riding buddy will always ensure you have someone to trust when riding. It also makes sure you are not left behind. If you see something strange or not safe, say something. Chaos can erupt in group rides, and dangerous riding in groups creates high risk. Stay away from any dangerous rider and talk about it at the next stop. If you still don't feel safe about it, ride with others.

The wave

You may have noticed that riders wave to each other when riding. They extend their left hand down low in a peace sign or a full hand wave. Why is this? For the simple reason of riding. In North America and other developed areas, we ride motorcycles for fun. Most of the world rides them out of necessity. When we go for a ride, it is to enjoy life and experience the wonder of two-wheel transportation. Naturally, we want to share this experience with other riders. This is where the wave comes in. A wave, peace sign, or whatever simple gesture will do. There is nothing complicated about it. If you see a rider coming the other way, wave. That's it. It does not matter what they ride.

In cities, waving happens less, as people are busy with their lives and maybe don't even know the wave. You'll also notice that scooter riders don't wave or that you feel strange waving to them. A scooter is technically a motorcycle, but it is quite different, too. In cities, waving can be quite inconsistent. Once you get outside city limits, you'll find waving is consistent. This is the open road, what it is all about. On sunny days on a popular road, your hand will be busy waving to all the happy riders you pass by. Embrace the wave. The simple wave shows the community riding has amongst the big, anonymous world of the road. We ride motorcycles and that unites us as a community.

Big social rides and events

If you're looking for big group rides and big social circles, go to the biggest events. Bike nights and charity rides are common in all riding communities. You'll have to register for the charity rides, and the cost usually includes prizes and food. It is a win-win, as you get to ride, meet new riders, and find new roads. These are not go-fast rides; they are good for cruising. Bike nights are a social night. You just show up with a motorcycle and chat with other riders. It is that simple. It is an evening or a day event that lasts a few hours. You'll get to check out several motorcycles and meet all sorts of riders. These events are the fastest way to meet and engage with the riders you want to ride with.

On these big rides, it is even more important to ride your own ride and respect everyone else's space and motorcycle. Some choose not to ride with big groups, as they feel they have too many riders. While one rider can spoil it for others, most riders are very respectful. Use your judgment, and as you get to know the community, you'll find the riders who are your favourites.

No drama!

Once you get into a group ride, this is where the real fun begins. I love this aspect of riding. It is what supercharged my experience. It also allowed me to move on from my old, stale high-school friends and into the ultra cool rider crowd. Soon I was having lifetime experiences with my new rider friends. We still talk about these experiences in our many reminiscing chats. Not all rides are perfect. Anytime you bring several people together, there are bound to be personal clashes.

I've been on more than one ride that hasn't gone smoothly. The more people you have, the more likely drama will occur. How that drama is handled is key. One particular ride I remember was my MotoGP trip to Laguna Seca. My riding buddy was with me the whole way from Vancouver to Laguna Seca Raceway in California. I was working as a corner worker, and he was a spectator. It was a three-day event and in the middle of it, he decided to leave early, leaving me on my own. I complained loudly but only over text message, so it was a highly unsatisfying way to vent my frustration. I sat alone in the restaurant. Here I was, at an event with over 100,000 people, and I was solo. It sucked. Not one to dwell on the change of plans, I instead became much more social. I was camping at the track and soon made friends with the people around me. Before I knew it, I was in a camper watching *On Any Sunday* (excellent motorcycle documentary from 1971) with others. We then went into Monterey for the bike night. It was packed with people and bikes, more than I've ever seen. My new group of friends were all from the California area and beyond. The next day I started to find other local riders from my home. They were riding back to Vancouver after the race, just like me. I managed to talk them into riding some incredible roads that were on my list. In the end I was forced to get out of my shell and meet new people, and my ride turned out even better. It is so true that we thrive when change is forced upon us. So what happened to the rider that ditched me? We worked it out, as time heals all. Glad I did, as we ended up riding through Mexico and several US states years later.

Drama is a common factor in any group. Roll with it, get over yourself, and enjoy the trip. Not everyone you ride with is easy to get along with. Don't be the one to elevate the drama to ridiculous levels. If you can't handle it, you always have your own motorcycle to ride off on. Just let your group know.

Riding solo vs. in groups

Riding a motorcycle is how you want to do it. It is ultimate independence. If the idea of a group ride scares you, that's OK. It is not for everyone. It is the best way to meet new riders, but you can still be social and ride solo, too. Whichever road you take, be friendly and open. Riders are the minority of traffic, so we have to look out for each other. If you ever need help, your rider buddies will be the first ones there.

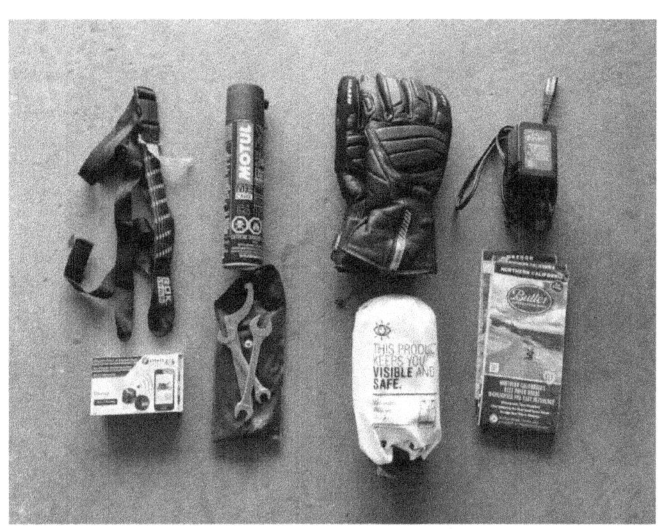

Chapter FOUR

Items a Rider Cannot Live Without

All you need for a motorcycle ride is you, your motorcycle, and some cash. That's it. That's how it used to be. Now riders are kitted out with all the latest technology and safety gear. You'll have more options than you know what to do with. So let's break it down and see what you really need.

Here comes the rain...

Rain gear is at the top of the list because you'll get wet quickly when the rains come. You don't need fancy motorcycle-specific rain gear, though. You can use any sort of rain shell that fits over your motorcycle gear. That's the key: that it fits over your motorcycle jacket. Try on rain gear with your gear on. You have the choice between rain suits and rain jackets. Both work, but the suit takes up more room. I prefer the jacket, and I'll deal with having wet pants.

Gloves and boots both come in waterproof form. GORE-TEX is your best bet. It will keep you warm, too. This does mean you'll need to have a second set. This can be expensive and unnecessary, especially with boots. I skip the waterproof boot and go right for the perforated boot. So yes, my feet get wet, but the airflow makes them dry more quickly. With a wool pair of socks, your feet will not get cold. A solid boot that gets wet will stay wet for days.

All rain gear has a time limit, so expect to get wet unless you are going to wear your scuba-diving dry suit. When you're riding at speed, the wind and rain have a habit of getting through. Another tip is to try to tuck closer to your motorcycle when it rains. The rain will reach less of you. If you're lucky, you'll barely get wet.

If it is a big rain storm, you are just going to have to ride through it. Be warned, the moment the rain wets your crotch, you will be wet for the rest of the day. Ah, the joys of motorcycling....

It's cold out here, but it's summer!

Every motorcycle rider should have heated gear. You'll be cold on your motorcycle more than you think, even in the middle of summer. I never leave home without my heated gear. Whenever I forget it or assume it'll be hot out, nature laughs at me. I've ridden in Baja, Mexico, with my heated gear on because of the cold wind coming in off the Pacific Ocean. I have ridden through central California mid-summer when an unseasonable weather pattern rolled through. Mid-summer is also very cold on the coast, as the hot summer temperatures pull in fog from the ocean. I cannot recommend a heated jacket and heated grips enough.

So how do they work? You'll need to install a cable to your motorcycle's battery. This is done by removing the seat and locating the battery. You'll see the red and black terminals. With a screwdriver, remove the screws and attach the heated gear cable. Reattach and tighten the screws, and you're done. It is just a matter of routing the cable to the outside of your seat. This will be the plug-in for your jacket and all of your other heated gear. This is a very simple install. You can do it.

The heated jacket is most important. You'll get heat through the arms, body, and even collar of the jacket. A heated vest works, too, but your arms will be quite exposed to the cold wind. Having warm arms keeps your hands warmer, too. Most heated jackets come with a heating control unit – always buy these ones. You will need various levels of heat. On a cold day, your heated gear will be worth its weight in gold.

Heated gloves or heated grips? Having heated gloves is good, but it is another pair of gloves to own, plus something else to plug in. Heated grips are a relatively simple install, and then you'll have heat on demand when you need it. The pure ease of heated grips makes this an easy choice. You can also choose the level of heat with nicer models. Having cold hands makes it harder to use your controls, and they're a constant distraction. Keep your hands warm so you can use them as you need them.

You also have the option of heated pants, heated shoe insoles, and even heated seats. These are nice, but they are not necessary. Having all this heated gear can get in the way, and you'll find heated grips, jacket, and some warm layers to be good enough.

All this heat does put a strain on your electrical system. A motorcycle's electrical system is designed to satisfy the needs of the motorcycle and maybe a few electrical components. Manufacturers have come to understand this, so you can safely add some electrical components to your motorcycle. Just know that every motorcycle has its limits with the power it can provide. Your battery is key to this as well. Motorcycle batteries are smaller, and the power draw of other electrical components can drain them quickly when the bike is not running.

Tools to ride with

Almost every motorcycle comes with a tool kit (a Harley-Davidson will not). These small tool kits are excellent at the basic needs and most maintenance requirements. If you ever find a bolt or screw loose on your motorcycle, find your kit and tighten it up. Most of them are located under the passenger seat, sometimes under the rider's seat. There are even tools in the kit to tighten and maintain your chain or adjust your suspension. All riders should ride with a tool kit.

A basic tool kit is enough, but having some extra tools is a great idea if you like riding with others or helping others. Those extra tools come in handy. You'll save the day for a rider or earn yourself a lunch. I carry a near-full set of tools. This may sound like a lot, but I have managed to squeeze these into a plastic case the size of a Kleenex box. It even has a tire plug kit in it.

The tire plug kit is a must. It is a frustrating experience to get a flat on a motorcycle. You should be able to plug the tire and be on your way if you have the right kit. Most automotive stores have the kit, so pick it up and try plugging a tire as soon as you can. Don't try to learn it roadside. Find a tire you can drive a nail into and practice it at least once. It is harder than it seems but much easier when you have already done it once before. Once you're done, getting the air back into the tire is the last step. Your options are a mini air compressor, mini hand pump, and CO_2 cartridges. The smallest is the mini hand pump. Yes, you will be pumping for a while, but you will get there. CO_2 cartridges work well but can be dangerous. If you have the space, go for the mini air compressor. It'll hook up right to your battery.

Since I started carrying around a tire plug kit, I have helped plug more tires than my own. You really save the day when you have a tire plug kit that someone needs. Anytime I have helped someone out (a friend or someone stranded on the side of the road), they generally return the favour with $20 cash. So in a way, my tire plug kit is making me money. The one time I did use it myself was during a weekend (when shops are closed) in the middle of nowhere, Washington. It was something I could take care of on the side of the road. My buddies had the mini air compressor, and I was back on my way in twenty minutes or less. That could have ended my road trip.

You should also know that local laws may prevent you from plugging a motorcycle tire. Most shops and dealers won't do it either. So it is entirely your choice to plug a tire. Is it even safe to ride on a motorcycle tire that is plugged? The answer really depends on the kind of puncture. There is no clear yes-or-no answer. From personal experience, I think it is fine, but I will check the tire more frequently after I plug it. If I have any doubt in my mind about the tire, I will replace it. It is not worth risking my safety.

Chain lube

Your motorcycle is full of moving parts. Oil and lubrication are mandatory. While an oil change is every 5,000 km (3,000 miles), your motorcycle chain needs a good spray every 1,000 km (600 miles). If it rains, spray it even more frequently. Every time you twist the throttle, your chain gets pulled with immense strength. That's what is propelling you forward at that thrilling speed. As the chain rolls around, your sprockets move a lot. Keeping the chain well-lubricated ensures it moves smoothly and keeps you safe. A neglected chain will dry, rust, stretch, and eventually break. Breaking chains create a very violent moment. Your chain could harmlessly shoot away from the bike. In my case, the chain smashed the engine with the force of a million towel snaps, blowing a hole in my engine. Your ride (and maybe your bike) will be over. You do not want to be around when a chain breaks. If it can blow a hole in my engine, don't even imagine what it could do your foot or leg. Take care of your chain.

The easiest way to take care of your chain is to buy a rear stand or something that can lift up the rear tire allowing you to spin it. While it's spinning, you can spray the chain much more easily. Depending on how hard it is to spray your chain, it could be a messy job. Wear gloves and use a rag to clean up any excess. Watch some YouTube videos on how it's done.

Keeping the bugs off your face

As you ride down the road, you'll also ride right through untold amounts of bugs. You will have to clean your visor off. Anything will do, but there are better products out there to keep your visor lasting longer. Every time you clean the visor, you will rub surface scratches into it. At the end of the season, the sun will highlight every one of these scratches.

I love using Pledge. It comes in a big can or disposable wipes. I opt for the wipes, as they are easier to travel with. Pledge has a thicker wax-like substance, so it does protect the visor better. Once you clean the surface, it is incredibly smooth and bugs slide off beautifully. It also makes cleaning easier and leaves you smelling lemon-fresh. There are motorcycle-specific cleaners, and they work great, too. But the value you get with Pledge is excellent.

Always carry a microfiber cloth or something similar. Spray the visor and let it sit there for a moment. Dried-on bugs can scratch your visor. When cleaning, move the cloth up and down gently. The more vigorously you clean, the more scratches you can embed into the visor. Having a clear visor is wonderful, especially a new one. Keep it optically perfect with some gentle care and patience when cleaning.

Recording your precious moments

A GoPro camera or something similar is not quite essential, but it is popular. A lot of riders keep one recording at all times to catch offending drivers. This can be good for insurance purposes. Placement for your camera is tricky. Putting it on your helmet adds weight and wind drag but shows your point of view. This placement is the most interesting. Placing it on your motorcycle keeps it in a fixed location. It is harder to watch a video from a stationary point. You'll soon see why motorcycles have multiple mounting points for their cameras. It is hard to choose.

The best camera is the one that is easy to use. Having one button to start and stop the video is key, and the GoPro Session is great for that. The more steps you have, the more videos you'll miss. You'll also need a big memory card to record so much video. If you are recording to make videos, keep in mind that the more you record, the more time you'll need to process the footage. Video editing can be **very** time consuming. Take advantage of the simple video apps out there. The one I like the most is GoPro Quik. It makes things very easy for everyone.

Cash is king

When it comes to problems or a surprise, you'll get the best deal with cash. Cash is king. Bring as much as you're comfortable with. Use it in emergencies. If you have to pay a mechanic for some quick work, nothing beats the ease and simplicity of cash. Think of it as a win-win. You get a better deal (most likely) and the mechanic gets some bonus work.

Cash is also the best identity-theft protection. Your personal info and bank accounts cannot get stolen with cash. You're travelling and going to places that may not be the most reputable. Leaving your credit card behind in some bar can add unnecessary stress to your trip. Credit cards and other forms of payment have their place. Use what you're comfortable with but always have the cash-reserve ready for the unexpected surprises the open road will bring you.

Earplugs and custom earplugs

Do not leave home without earplugs. Your helmet does not eliminate harmful wind noise. Some helmets are better than others, but there is no helmet that will protect your ears. An all-day ride at highway speeds will damage your hearing over time. Riding around the city is fine.

On the highway, the decibels can reach eighty-five. It is the same amount of noise from busy city traffic or a hair dryer. This is where hearing damage begins. Your ears may tolerate noise for a time, but at the end of the day, you won't feel great. The faster you go the louder the wind noise gets. Motorcycle riding on the highway can easily exceed 100 db, especially with a loud exhaust. If you're exposed to 100 db for longer than fifteen minutes, you will damage your ears in a shorter amount of time. When we're exposed to loud noises, it agitates us. We don't relax. When things quiet down or are muted, now we can focus and relax. This is the mindset we need when riding. With a good pair of earplugs, you'll be much calmer.

Ear plugs are cheap, so there is no good reason not to wear them. They really do make for a more pleasurable riding experience and reduce fatigue. You will be able to ride longer with hearing protection. This also means you are alone with your thoughts for your entire ride. For some, this might not be a good thing. If you cannot hear anything, you might as well listen to music. This is where those great Bluetooth devices (Cardo, Sena, etc.) come in. On long, straight sections of road, I'll start a podcast and enjoy that, too.

You can also go one step further and go for custom-fit earplugs. They take a mold of your ear and create a set that fits your ears exactly. If you want to get fancy, you can get them made with a headset installed. Now you have custom earplugs with the ability to listen to music and other riders, the best solution out there. It can be expensive, but it is worth it. Just don't lose them.

Things have gone horribly wrong and now who do you contact?

If you need to contact the loved one of a rider in your group, how are you going to do it? The person may be your best riding buddy in the world, but you probably don't know who to contact if they need help. Always ensure someone (or everyone) in your group has your emergency contact info. Paramedics know this as In Case of Emergency (ICE) information. They are trained to look for it on your phone. However, most phones are locked. Both iPhone and Android phones have the ability to enter your emergency contacts. They also go one step further on cell phones. You'll be able to enter medications, allergies, blood type, height, and weight. This can be critical information in a critical moment. You can also take it one step further and have it as part of your lock screen via the wallpaper. It is still a good idea to have a paper copy, however, as your cell phone could be damaged, especially if you crash.

Tracking your ride

It can be concerning to your family when you go off for a ride. You can offer them some peace of mind in the form of tracking. Google Maps allows you to track your location. A SPOT transponder will do the same but will cost you. A small Bluetooth tracker like Tile will also work. These are great ways to let your family know where you are. If you were to disappear, they would know your last known location.

Since most cell phones have GPS capabilities, the Google Maps location feature can be enabled from your cell phone. It can accelerate battery loss and incur extra data charges. This can be the cheapest form of tracking or the most expensive, depending upon your cell phone plan. The SPOT transponder or something similar is a small device you bring with you. It has a few simple buttons allowing you to check in every day, and if things go wrong, you can issue a 911 call for rescue. This has the most options, and you don't have to rely on anyone else to come rescue you. Keep it attached to you and not your bike.

The Bluetooth tracker Tile works very well if it is near your cell phone or other Tile members. All you need to do is purchase one and connect it to your phone, and you're good to go. It's not as accurate as a GPS, but close enough to find you if necessary.

Everything and the kitchen sink

Last but not least, a first aid kit or medical kit. These come in all shapes and sizes. Bring one that works with your luggage space. Having a few band aids, alcohol wipes and even Benadryl for insect stings can be extremely helpful. On motorcycle trips I have taken a bungie cord to the face, cut myself changing a fuse, and been stung by a wasp more than once. A good band aid is worth Its weight in gold at the right moment.

You can easily get carried away with too much stuff and you really do not need much when going on a motorcycle trip. Plan ahead for the worst-case scenario, but don't go overboard, as the odds of something bad happening are still low. A little bit of preparation goes a long way.

Chapter FIVE

Motorcycle Modifications and Suspension

Your motorcycle is yours and what you do with it is up to you. Your motorcycle can be an extension of you. Go ahead and make it into your vision. By the time you're done, you'll have a one-of-a-kind machine that you may value as much as your kids. That should seem silly, but given the level of involvement and love some riders have for their motorcycles, I am inclined to believe it.

Before we go down the rabbit hole of modifications and suspension, there is something you should consider: your warranty. Some modifications can void your warranty. Consult your dealer first and explain what you want to do. You may have to restore back to its stock form in order to get warranty service. If it is out of warranty, then the sky's the limit. Do what you wish.

The best modifications you can do

Suspension, your motorcycle's seat, and luggage options are some of the best modifications you can do. They will make your motorcycle perform better in the corners (important!), make it more comfortable to ride, and allow you to bring a few things with you. They will also help retain the value of your motorcycle. Suspension is one of the most overlooked mods to do. The stock suspensions are usually designed for someone weighing 150 lbs. Given that the average North American male weighs in at 178 lbs., your stock suspension is probably ill-equipped to deal with your weight. It'll handle just fine, but it could handle a lot better. Those who have good suspensions and proper tuning know. A suspension that is tuned to the rider changes the motorcycle dramatically. You'll be at one with your motorcycle and it will feel like it knows the corners before you even get there.

The easiest and cheapest thing you can do is see a suspension specialist. For around $50, they will explain your suspension and adjust it to your weight and riding style. If your motorcycle's suspension is limited, they can make suggestions on how to improve it. I cannot recommend this enough and only a small percentage of riders actually look at their suspension. Having your suspension setup correctly does add safety to your ride, too. Reading your manual and visiting a suspension specialist can benefit you a lot.

Whether you already have advanced suspension or you upgrade to it, you really need to see a specialist. Given the complexity of suspensions and how adjustments can affect every other type of adjustment, only suspensions professionals should adjust them. Suspension tuning is a Black Art. If you don't believe me, go view videos done by the legend Dave Moss. I've been fortunate enough to have my suspension tuned by him at the track. He can have one look at your tire and tell you how your suspension reacts to the road. Then he can make adjustments and recommendations. And there are plenty of guys like Dave out there in the world who can take care of your motorcycle's suspension. It is truly my favourite thing to adjust or modify on my motorcycle.

Your motorcycle seat and handlebars can change the riding position and comfort of your motorcycle. Stock motorcycle seats can be comfortable, but they are limited to their design. Some motorcycles are narrower than others and the padding can be quite lacking. This is true for all motorcycles but especially sport bikes. Sport bikes are not designed to be comfortable. For that reason, there are specially designed motorcycle seats and customizers that will make your motorcycle much more comfortable. If you decide to go touring on your motorcycle, you'll see most riders have custom seats. Corbin, Sargent, and Saddlemen are the big companies, but there are small, local independents out there, too. In addition to the added comfort, you get a custom design, which will really make your motorcycle stand out. Extra comfort and better looks—that's a win. The handlebars or clip-ons can also be changed. With some models, it will be quite difficult, but most can accept a new set. Anything sporty benefits from this change. For example, I love sport bikes but my size and height make them uncomfortable for long rides. It can almost feel like you're doing a complicated yoga position. When I've changed the bars, I can sit more upright. My comfort level is good for the day, and I find I am better rider. The leaning-over sport position is great for the track and feeling sporty. It won't do well for the long straight roads or rush-hour traffic. If you're like me and love sport bikes but can't quite get comfortable riding them, consider changing the bars or clip-ons. The same can be done for your feet in a more limited way. You might be able to replace the foot pegs or rear sets, which will allow your feet to sit lower. Your legs will not be so cramped up. These mods can be expensive so choose your motorcycle wisely.

You may wonder how much a motorcycle can carry. Most can carry what you can fit on your body. There used to be room beneath the passenger seat. With all the new designs, that room has been eliminated. Tank bags, tail bags, or even saddlebags are your best options. A tank bag attaches to your tank using magnets or straps. A tail bag attaches via straps as do saddlebags. You can even get a rack fitted to your motorcycle for even more storage options. The size of the bag determines how much you can bring. If it is a short ride, you really don't need anything. For longer trips or anything in less-than-ideal weather, a visor cleaner, a cloth, a rain jacket, heated gear, a tire plug kit, house keys, sunglasses, and some water are essentials. If you find yourself stuffing your pockets with all this stuff, just keep in mind that you might be falling on it.

These three modifications offer the biggest value for your money. They change the ride to something comfortable and even more capable. They may not be what you thought of doing right away, but if you are serious about riding, these will make the biggest difference. If you get the opportunity, ride a motorcycle with great suspension, comfort, and luggage space. Once you do, it's tough to ride anything else.

The mods you should really wait on or ignore

Changing out the stock exhaust is the go-to mod for most riders. For as little as $300, a slip-on exhaust is an easy install and will change the look and sound of the motorcycle. Gone will be that oversized can it came with; some stock exhausts can really go against the look of the motorcycle. An aftermarket exhaust can change your motorcycle into a loud beast, angry at everything. It really changes the sound, and part of that change is noise. You will exceed the legal allowable limit, which will annoy almost everyone around you and likely earn you a ticket. While I am a fan of aftermarket exhausts (I have one myself), the noise they generate can be obnoxious. It is up to you to be respectful and reasonable about it. Only you and your riding buddies will enjoy it. Those who will not include your neighbours, pedestrians, and cops. Please do not fully rev or accelerate up hills, over bridges, or through neighbourhoods. Save that for the track, quiet roads, and desert rides. The ironic thing about loud exhausts is that the rider usually wears hearing protection, so they really can't hear how loud they are. This is one of the big reasons motorcycle riders get a bad reputation. We're excessively loud. And if you think all that noise is good for your safety, think again. Traffic doesn't always move for police cars, ambulances, or fire trucks with their lights and sirens blazing. How are they going to hear your exhaust, especially when it is pointed away from the direction you're going? Yes, there are some safety benefits of a loud exhaust, but they are minimal and inconsistent. Ride as if your motorcycle makes no noise at all. Lastly, it will do nothing for your ability to ride. The horsepower increase is negligible. New riders should spend this money on advanced rider training, as that will add more performance to your motorcycle than any exhaust will.

You can take it one step further by installing a full exhaust system. Cost can easily exceed $1,000. Instead of a slip on, this is a pipe that goes from the engine and all the way to the end. This is a much bigger modification than the easy-to-add slip on. You'll have to get the computer updated (or a power commander installed), as the new exhaust system will change how gas is consumed and exhausted. Your motorcycle was designed with the exhaust system it came with. Changing the entire thing does require new software and even hardware. Consult your chosen performance shop and do some homework about what is involved. Since this is a bigger mod to do, you will get more of a horsepower benefit. It still comes with all the noise, but you do get a cleaner look and weight savings. It'll remove the catalytic converter, for example, which can weigh 10 to 20 lbs. on its own. There are clear benefits of having a lighter motorcycle, but those benefits are for the track or the very experienced rider.

Other mods you should seriously stay away from are the ones that permanently change your motorcycle. This could be welding things onto it, drilling unnecessary holes, or adding anything of cheap quality. Be very careful if you change the tire size or anything that can affect the handling. There is very little value to doing these sorts of mods. They are more likely to turn potential purchasers away. Even mods like good suspension don't add the value they should. The motorcycle that is fully stock is the easiest to sell.

Great mods to do on a budget

There are small cosmetics you can add to your motorcycle that will make it stand out. One of my favorites is rim tape. This strip of colour can really make your wheels stand out and match the colour of your motorcycle or your gear. Your clear windscreen can also be changed to something smoked, black, or reflective. This is an easy mod for most motorcycles. Your levers can be changed to be adjustable. The Pazzo Racing company is a pioneer in this, but there are also lots of knock offs out there. Adjustable levers are great for hands of all sizes. They come in different colours, so you can match them to whatever you want. A tail tidy or a fender eliminator takes the oversized rear license-plate holder and makes it much more streamlined. The stock license plate holders are ugly additions that are mandatory for legality, so removing them can put your motorcycle offside. The replacement you buy will look 100 times better, but you do risk a ticket if the police officer does not like it. Decals, stickers, and even plastidip (removable plastic spray paint) will make you look as if you have a sponsorship. This may be the look you are going for. If not, a few in the right place work great.

Your motorcycle is an extension of you

The more you ride, the more the motorcycle becomes an extension of you. It becomes a window to your personality. Full motorcycle gear changes the look of who you are. Your gear and motorcycle become your alter ego. This is all part of the fun and excitement of riding. You'll love your motorcycle even more doing the right mods that work for you. Sometimes the manufacturers completely nail the look, so no mods are required. They can be pieces of artwork worthy of a place in your home.

Chapter SIX

Maintenance and Mechanics

Just like everything mechanical, your motorcycle will need to be maintained. The good news is that you don't need to be a mechanic to take care of your motorcycle. In my first book, I covered the basics. I'll cover those again and expand on them even more.

Motorcycles are tough and can handle quite a bit of neglect. This can give you a false sense of security. And your motorcycle will indeed be fine, until it is not. When it breaks, it will not be convenient, either. I can promise you that it takes a minimal amount of effort to take care of your motorcycle. It is one of those tasks that becomes easier and easier the more you do it.

There are three great resources for maintaining your motorcycle. The first is your motorcycle manual. This will list the services required at every milestone you hit on your odometer. For example, the BMW 310R requires its first service at 1,200 km (800 miles) and then a service every 10,000 km (6,000 miles). Newer models can have very simple maintenance intervals. Older models may require maintenance every 5,000 km (3,000 miles). This handy section of your manual is worthy of a bookmark. You can also consult online motorcycle forums for your specific motorcycle. There is one for every motorcycle model, so you will be able to see what other people are experiencing with their motorcycles. The third resource is YouTube. If you ever want to learn how to perform maintenance tasks, then simply search for what you need to do. If anything seems too complicated for you, go see your local mechanic and make good friends with them.

If you really want to know more about your motorcycle and maintaining it, take a simple motorcycle maintenance course. Ask motorcycle dealers, shops, and schools when they are being offered. They can cost as little as $50. If you cannot find one where you live, consider hiring a mechanic to show you the basics. The cost of a motorcycle maintenance course can easily pay for itself after you do a couple of oil changes yourself. You'll also be able to diagnose small problems and possibly take care of them yourself. There is certainly a sense of pride in taking care of your motorcycle. A well-maintained motorcycle is a safe motorcycle.

The small stuff

So what about all the stuff in between the service intervals? Good news: there's not much to do, especially on a newer motorcycle. Every couple of rides (every three rides or every two weeks), you should you should check the oil, check the tire pressure, check the chain, and look for leaking fluids. My favourite acronym for taking care of my motorcycle is TCLOCK. It is taught my school (and others) and is excellent for checking over a motorcycle you want to buy.

T – Tires

C – Controls

L – Lights

O – Oil

C – Chassis and chain

K – Kickstand

Tires. The two points that connect you to the road. Very important. Check the surface of the tire and look for any nails, metal, or wear on the tire. You want a clean tire with lots of life left in it. If you are getting close to the wear bars (indicators of tire life), then order a new set and get them replaced. Please don't push the life of your tire. You might be riding on limited traction. Next check the air pressure of the tire. Find a tire-pressure gauge and keep it with you. Keep your tire pressure close to the manual recommendations. If you are lazy about this, buy yourself a tire-pressure monitoring system. They can be had for as little as $50 online. I love mine. It makes it easy for me to keep the tires perfectly inflated. This saves me money and keeps me safe. If

I make it easy to do, I will do it. The easiest way to top up air pressure is with a bicycle pump. Adding a little air is a small task for a bicycle pump. If you are ever curious about how old your tire is, find the four-digit code on the side of the tire. If it says 1017, it means the tire was made in the tenth week of 2017. Motorcycle tires shouldn't be used if they are five years old or older, although opinions vary wildly on the lifespan of motorcycle tires. Just remember that the older they are, the less traction they provide. Rubber hardens as it ages.

Controls. Anything your hands or feet touch should be checked. The clutch and brake levers should work nicely. If they move around a little bit, that is OK. Check the bolts and screws around them to ensure they have not loosened. Twist the throttle back and see if it snaps back to position. If it doesn't, things could get exciting on a ride. Turn the handle bars back and forth to see if they move freely. If you installed heated grips or new lights, the new wiring might restrict the movement of the bars. For your feet, give the rear brake lever a few presses. The shifter will move around a bit and that is OK. Have a closer look at it, as there are more moving parts to it. You certainly want to find any problems with your controls now and not on your ride.

Lights. Other traffic needs to see you easily, so don't leave home without your lights shining bright. Check the taillights so that traffic can see you slowing down. The taillight should light up when either the front brake or rear brake is used. Check the signals and, of course, the headlights, high beam and low beam. If only one headlight illuminates, it doesn't necessarily mean you have a burnt-out headlight; it probably means your high beam is the other headlight. Very common for sport bikes. Motorcycle batteries and electrical systems are smaller and they all can't handle the power required for two headlights. Adding more lights can be a good idea for visibility, but stay within legal limits. Only use white and amber lights shining forward and red or amber lights shining rear. Any other colors are probably illegal for public roads.

Oil. Checking the oil is straightforward. First find where the oil goes. It is usually a twist-off cap that looks like a drain plug. It is located on the right side of the motorcycle, towards the bottom. Below that and near the bottom of the motorcycle, you should see a window. It will be the size of your pocket change. When the motorcycle is leaned over, it should be clear. When the motorcycle is upright, oil should flow in and cover two-thirds of the window. It might be a good idea to get someone to hold up the motorcycle while you check. It can be tricky to hold up the motorcycle and look at the sight window on your own. If you cannot see any oil, top it up with whatever oil your motorcycle manual recommends. Only use motorcycle-specific oil.

Chassis and chain. Walk around your motorcycle and look for anything out of the ordinary. Maybe someone bumped into it, knocked it over, and picked it up again. You'd want to know. This is also a good time to check for leaking fluids. If your motorcycle leaks oil (brown fluid) or coolant (green fluid), get it checked out as soon as you can. Your motorcycle might "leak" water. This is condensation dripping off the motorcycle. Don't worry about it. Before you're done your walk around, get up close and personal with your motorcycle chain. I consider this to be the most-used part, and it's under the most stress. Every time you twist the throttle, it gets pulled with an immense amount of torque. That's why it's heavy duty. This chain needs to be relatively clean and well-lubricated at all times.

For those of your with a belt drive system on your motorcycle. It still needs inspection. Look closely at the belt for any tears, broken teeth, or damage. Be sure to inspect the pulley as well. This pulls the belt along. You'll only ever have to do every oil change but checking it more often won't hurt either. Some belts can last up to 160,000kms/100,000 miles! If you have a shaft drive then no maintenance needed. It needs its gear oil replaced every 40,000kms/25,000 miles.

Kickstand. The simplest part of your check-over. Make sure the kickstand moves freely and when kicked up, stays up. You can also check the spring the kickstand Is attached too. If that ever breaks or falls off then the kickstand will not stay up. If this is a problem having some twine or some zap straps will come in handy for a temporary fix. There is also a small wire that can come loose or become frayed. This is a sensor that, when triggered, may shut the bike off. It ensures you do not ride away with the kickstand down.

If you run this check regularly, you'll rarely deal with any problems on the road.

Working with mechanics

You've got two options: the mechanic at the dealer or the independent mechanic. Both will get the job done, but what matters most is how good they are, their reputation.

Dealer mechanics are a good option for a new motorcycle. All new motorcycles require a first service, and the warranty may require it as well. When a motorcycle is shipped to a dealer, it comes mostly assembled with no fluids. It is the dealer's job to put the motorcycle together. This is called PDI on your invoice. Your first service is usually done after the first 1,000 km (600 miles). They'll change the oil and make sure all the bolts are still tight. The dealer knows your new motorcycle better than anyone, so the first service should be done there.

The following service needs can be met by almost any mechanic. The dealer will welcome your business, but it might be above the average cost. They have to meet higher requirements set out by the brand they represent. They also use original equipment manufacturer parts, and these can cost more, too. You are paying for a higher level of service, so it is fair to expect it.

Booking your motorcycle for an appointment isn't always convenient. Dealers can be very busy. When motorcycle season starts or is in full swing, you will wait for a service appointment. Don't assume they can take you right away.

Working with an independent mechanic is your other option. Independent mechanics have their own shops or just work out of a garage. Because they are not attached to a brand or dealer, their reputation is very important. Ask around and check out reviews to see if they are worthy of your business. Costs are lower with these mechanics. Since they don't have to pay as much for their shop space and licenses, the savings are passed on to you. Pay your service bills with cash—mechanics love cash.

Independent mechanics are great for the basic services such as oil, brakes, tires, and anything requiring an hour or two of service. For anything major, it would be best to ask some questions to see how qualified the mechanic is. Most mechanics are more familiar with certain motorcycles and work than they are with others. Often, they are passionate motorcyclists. They are taking their love of motorcycles and making it their life. You'll quite often see some cool projects they are working on.

Whichever option you go with – independent, dealer, or both – be nice to your mechanic. They are working on your motorcycle and will work much better if you give them the time to do it. That said, you can hold them to the day your motorcycle is supposed to be ready. If they make a mistake, hold them to it but don't fly into a rage. When you get your motorcycle back, check it over.

I once grabbed my motorcycle and rode off without the check-over. I've dealt with lots of mechanics over my years of riding and something will get missed, sooner or later. This is normal. Mechanics are humans, too, and not perfect. They will make some mistakes just like everyone else. As I rode away and began my ride to California, my motorcycle started to have a rather odd hum. I kept going for a little longer, but it persisted. I found a place to pull over and see what was up. It did not take me long to see that my rear brake caliper had fallen off and was only held on by the brake hose. The two bolts holding it together were not tightened enough, and they backed off, then fell off entirely. With the brake caliper dangling down, it was grinding up against my rear tire, causing the hum. Yikes. That could have been much worse. This was not something I could fix on the side of the road, so I removed the caliper and clamped off the hose so the brake fluid would not leak. Riding without a rear brake is not really a good idea, but you can get away with it. I rode to a nearby track day, which was full of motorcycles. I found a few people with enough skill to help me out. They found two new bolts, fixed my caliper, and attached it all back on. I was good to go. Had I done my check-over, I probably would have found this oversight. When I got back from California, I certainly had words with my mechanic over this. He was remorseful, and while I could have really ripped into him, there would have been no point. It's up to the mechanic to do the job right, but it is also up to me to check over my motorcycle. When you ride a motorcycle, you are always the one at risk.

Working on your motorcycle at home

Lots of basic maintenance can be done at home. Washing your motorcycle is the easiest. You may not consider this maintenance, but getting up close and personal with your motorcycle is the first step to good maintenance. You'll notice things missing or even some damage that you do not recognize. Having a clean motorcycle also shows the pride of your ownership. Best of all, with the right washing tools, you'll have cleaned it in no time at all.

My favourite cleaning tools are a paint brush, soft cloth, and bucket. Find yourself a giant paint brush from the dollar store or an unused one in your garage. Cover the metal parts of the brush with tape. Spray your motorcycle down with water and get that paint brush soapy. The bristles of the paint brush really get into all those hard-to-reach places. Thousands of tiny bristles are very efficient. The soft cloth can do the parts of the motorcycle that are easy to clean. Cleaning the wheels can be tougher, but having rear and front stands can make things easier.

If you want to change the oil, find the largest bolt at the bottom of the motorcycle. You may have to remove some of the plastics or engine guards to get at it. Once you find and unscrew it, oil will flow out of there quite quickly. So before doing that, get an oil pan or a tinfoil turkey pan from the dollar store. It is best to do this when the motorcycle engine is warm. Warm oil will flow better than cold. Now have a look at the bolt you unscrewed: there should be a metal washer (the thin donut). This ensures that the bolt goes on tight and nothing leaks out. It is best to have some spares so you can replace it if need be. If you do not have one, you can reuse it by flipping it over. If you are a mechanic reading this, you might be shaking your head in disapproval. I'll take it. I don't always have the spares, so I'll reuse them. I have yet to have a problem with this. Your motorcycle may have an oil filter as well. This is located just behind the front tire most of the time. When all the oil is out of the motorcycle, it is time to unscrew this. If you are strong, you can do it with your hands. If you need something extra you can buy the right tool or use a strap to help with the untightening. Replace the filter with every oil change. If you don't change it, make sure you change it next time. On a long road trip, I did a roadside oil change in front of Napa Auto Parts. Napa doesn't really like this, so maybe find somewhere else to do it. On the road, I want to keep things simple, so I don't change the oil filter. Again, the mechanics reading this might be screaming at the book right now. I'd rather have fresh oil and a "dirty" oil filter than dirty oil and a dirty filter. Finally, please dispose of your dirty oil properly. Almost any mechanic can dispose of the oil for you. Ask nicely.

Also check your chain. If it looks like a war zone, get some kerosene (camping fuel, which is a close relative of diesel fuel) and clean it. Consider avoiding the heavy-duty degreasers, as they can dry out the chain. The chain needs to be coated in a lubricant at all times. Every 1,000 km (600 miles), you should spray it with motorcycle chain lubricant. Don't have any? Buy some. If you still don't have any, use WD-40. Using WD-40 is not the best option, but it'll do just fine until you get the right stuff. Don't spray the motorcycle chain in the center, but rather in the small gap between the links. This is where the O-rings are, and they need the lubrication the most. The best time to spray your motorcycle chain is after a ride when it is warm. The easiest way to spray your motorcycle chain is with a rear stand. This lifts the tire and makes it easy. Taking care of your motorcycle chain can save you plenty of money, as motorcycle chains, sprockets, and mechanic labour can get expensive. If your motorcycle has a belt or shaft drive, then there is nothing you have to do other than have a good look at it and check for tears or fraying. Make sure you know when the belt should be changed and when your shaft drive needs the drive oil changed.

Your air filter is something that should be looked at once a year or more if you ride dusty roads. If you cannot easily find your air filter, it might be located beneath your fuel tank. Consult the manual to find it. There could be all sorts of things living in there. You'll find lots of dirt, bugs, and maybe even a family of mice. They have been known to crawl into the air vents and make a home. If your motorcycle is struggling, it may mean your motorcycle is not getting enough air. The air filter may be clogged.

Your battery is like a sponge. When it is brand new, it holds water very well. As it ages, it holds less and less water. Keep your battery in the best shape by always keeping it charged. This means plugging it into a charger when you are not using your motorcycle for longer than two weeks. If you have to recharge the battery too many times, it will stop holding a charge and you'll have to buy a new one. If you keep it charged, it can last you several years. If you don't want to keep it charged through the off season, unhook the battery and periodically charge it to keep it topped off. If you are curious about the quality of your battery, get a mechanic to do a load test. This is a fancy device that shows just how strong it is.

Motorcycle maintenance is not rocket science

Maintaining your motorcycle is a requirement for riding a motorcycle. If you just can't stand the thought of doing it yourself, build a good friendship with your mechanic and bring cash. They take care of the small stuff for you. Buying a new motorcycle will also lessen your maintenance needs. If you are up for some light dirty work, get some gloves and keep that bike maintained. You'll find it is just some effort and patience. You'll be rewarded with a well-running and safe motorcycle. This motorcycle will also get you top dollar when you go to sell it.

Chapter SEVEN

Crashing – Know the Stats

So why is crashing a motorcycle supposedly mandatory? I wondered that, too. I was very afraid of it. I saw others crash. Some were serious but most were minor. When my first crash happened, it wasn't that bad. I knew I didn't want to crash again, but I did. Thankfully, I have not crashed very much and most of it has been in advanced rider training with a few spills on the street. If you talk to riders, they will all have their own stories. As a motorcycle instructor, I cringe hearing about my students crashes. I am thankful they are mostly minor and that they'll share their story with me. It takes a lot of courage to do so. If you do happen to crash, treat it as your own fault. You're the rider, and you make the decisions. It is not random luck that some riders can ride all their lives and never have anything serious happen. You can ride motorcycles crash-free, but it is up to you.

We'll first dive into the statistics[1] of crashing. I covered this in my first book, *'Your First Motorcycle'* but we will go even further into them with updated figures. This will arm you with the knowledge on what to avoid or reduce.

------

[1] These stats are based on reports and studies from the Insurance Corporation of British Columbia, The Insurance Institute for Highway Safety, the National Highway Traffic Safety Administration, the National Transportation Safety Board, Virginia Polytechnic Institute, PubMed Central, and the George Institute for Global Health.

The big stats on motorcycle accidents

If you ride motorcycles, you are risking your life, but you can change how drastic that risk is. Generally, it's less than you think as long as you're smart about it. Just reading this book already puts you in the smarter category. We all get to hear the ugly stats of motorcycling, but when we pull back our view on them, it is much more of a three-dimensional view on what matters. The most common "go-to" motorcycle stat is a comparison to driving a car. The numbers vary depending on the study, but on average, you are thirty-five times more likely to have a fatal accident on a motorcycle than in a car, and you are five times more likely to get injured. That sounds awful. Remember that these stats include everyone, and a lot of people make bad decisions. That is not going to be you. We can't protect ourselves from all risk, but we can certainly reduce it to acceptable levels.

Let's cover the big ones. The big stats, the ones that deserve your attention, are alcohol use, intersections, and speeding. This is where you have a significant amount of control, so it is really up to you. Thirty-three per cent of motorcycle fatalities involve alcohol. The rider had one drink or more, got on their motorcycle and went for a ride. Even if your local laws allow you to have one or two drinks, do not do it. The stats do not lie. Make a promise to yourself to never drink and ride. Doing so will reduce your chance of killing yourself on a motorcycle by thirty-three per cent.

I've already mentioned that intersections are the most dangerous places to ride. It is well worth repeating. Treat these with the utmost respect and take it easy riding through them. A very common witness statement to police or paramedics is how fast the motorcycle was travelling before the crash. You should already know to slow down (slightly), do an extra check, and proceed with caution through all intersections. Where I live, there is only one insurance company. They handle it all, and 70 per cent (or more) of their claims are in intersections. Never take anything for granted with intersections. Use your common sense and trust no one. Speeding is difficult to control. I didn't buy my motorcycle to go the speed limit all the time, but I know that the more I speed, the more the odds are against me. Keeping your speed reasonable is easier said than done. Speed is thrilling and addictive. So you really have to pick your places on where you are going to speed. The best place for that is the track. It is the best way to get it out of your system. You'll also realize how silly it is to speed excessively on the street. Keep your speed reasonable.

These are the big three of motorcycle accidents. If these were the only stats you followed and respected, the odds of you crashing would go down significantly. But we're not going to stop here. Let's keep going deeper on how and why we can bring our risk down even further. I'm confident that riding a motorcycle can be as safe as driving a car.

Who you are and what you ride

Your age and the motorcycle you ride can determine how likely you are to crash. So who crashes the most? The answer is either males under the age of thirty on supersports or the over-fifty crowd on cruisers. It is actually worse for males under thirty. There are far more licensed riders over the age of fifty, and while they make up a big number of the stats, the ratio of crashes to riders is much higher for young supersport riders. A supersport rider can be four times more likely to crash than any other type of motorcyclist. This group is special for several reasons. The under-thirties are riding a motorcycle that is highly technical and in moments can go from quiet to insane speeds. Our brains just can't keep up with how quickly the motorcycle can move our bodies. Add in the bravado and excitement of a younger male and it is a recipe for disaster. So why do they even allow these motorcycles on the road? Well, there is nothing wrong with them. They are built for the race track and made street legal. The cool-factor and desire-factor determine the market, so they are here to stay. If you are in this category, start by buying a smaller supersport or take your motorcycle to the track — or both. If you are going to buy the full-size supersport, you need superhuman discipline. You'll also need to take several riding courses to know how to ride it. These are incredible machines with the latest in technology. You are not good enough to ride them (yet) and if you are, you still have to remember that they go well past the legal limits of public roads.

The over-fifty crowd is represented for completely different reasons. They ride mostly cruisers and there's nothing wrong with the motorcycle — it's the rider. The older we get, the slower our reactions become and the longer we take to heal. Most older riders are usually coming back after a hiatus from riding. This hiatus makes your skills rusty. You might still know how to ride, but you are not nearly as sharp as you were before. The good news is that it's easy to relearn, so take a course and get back into it. You need to have the beginner's mindset, even at an older age. Young or old, it does not matter because motorcycles do not discriminate. They demand respect at all times, regardless of the rider.

This doesn't mean everyone else is safe. If you are in your mid-thirties and riding a touring motorcycle, you are represented minimally in the stats. It is a good place to be, but it is still two wheels and you're exposed. We all still face the risks and the moment you take your skills for granted, the motorcycle will show you ground. Ask a few of my students taking my course: I crashed in front of them. It happens to the best of us, but in front of students, it was pretty embarrassing.

Women are the fastest-growing segment of motorcycle riders. They also have a great approach to risk. We all should have the same mindset women do when it comes to motorcycles. At Northwest Motorcycle School, they tell their students to "learn like a lady." Men like to see what a motorcycle can do; women want to learn how to ride it. This chasm of difference is why women will always crash less than men. When they do crash, it is typically at lower speeds, too. Women would benefit from having more confidence, as sometimes too little speed can be as risky as too much speed.

All motorcycles are dangerous to ride, but a special focus on supersports and big cruisers shows up in the stats. If you fall into the high-risk areas of age and motorcycle type, strongly consider choosing a different type of motorcycle. It might just make the difference for you. Later on, get the motorcycle you truly would love to have.

The safest times and days to ride

Every time is a good time to ride, but some times are better than others. The absolute worst time to ride a motorcycle is from late afternoon to evening. This is the time of day when everyone is getting tired, they're coming home from work, they could be stressed out, there's rush-hour traffic, it's getting dark, and many people have been drinking alcohol at happy hour. Plenty of factors to make your motorcycle ride much more dangerous. This is why the morning and early afternoon are much better times to ride. Everyone is more awake, alert, and sober. It is also light out and traffic is quieter. We never want to drop our guard riding motorcycles, but you will need extra vigilance riding later in the day. Riding at night is fine, but still not much safer than late afternoon. It is dark, you can't see the road as well, it is colder, and still more drivers have alcohol in their systems. Fewer motorcycle riders ride at night, so there is not enough data to show how much more dangerous it is.

Given the information we do know, it is safe to assume that daylight is the better way to go. My preferred time to ride is from 8:00 a.m. to late afternoon. On big trips, this is the sweet spot for risk. It is also the most enjoyable. On an overnight trip I took years ago, I left early in the morning to get to the lakeside campsite as early as possible. I had a great day in the sun. The next day I did not leave until the afternoon. I had two very different rides. On the ride out, I was fresh, excited, and full of energy. The next day, my ride home was slower and less energetic, and I just wanted to be home. This was a great comparison on how different we can be at different times of the day.

New safety technology

Everyone can crash spectacularly, technology or no technology, but I love all the new safety mechanisms in our motorcycles. They give me an extra edge in staying safe, and they are allowing more and more people to ride motorcycles.

The biggest technology gains in safety have been in anti-lock braking (ABS). It first debuted in 1988 on a BMW, but it wasn't readily available until the early 2000s. Even then, it was only on higher-end models. ABS has now been around long enough that it shows up in the statistics. The first to take notice was insurers. The rate of fatal crashes on motorcycles is 31 per cent lower on motorcycles with ABS, and collision insurance claims are filed 20 per cent less often. These are huge numbers showing increasing safety. It makes getting a motorcycle without ABS a hard choice. Cornering ABS is now available on higher-end motorcycles, as well. Standard ABS won't help you in the corners, but cornering ABS will. When the motorcycle is leaned over, the computers calculate the maximum amount of brakes to be used based on wheel speed and lean angle. Complicated stuff. Hammering the brakes mid-corner is a big problem for motorcycles. We just tend to lose our skill set when panicking. Cornering ABS will lower the fatality and accident stats for motorcycles again.

Traction control is another beautiful safety measure for motorcyclists. While there is no hard data on how effective it is, it is still early. My 2011 Kawasaki ZX10R had traction control, and I did benefit from it. It reads the traction of the tire 300 times per second. So that one time on the track I leaned over a little too far and gave it too much gas, traction control stepped in. It eased the throttle off the moment I was losing traction. It was a scary moment, but it saved the day. I am a big fan of traction control for this reason. In a few years, we will have statistical data supporting my experience.

The last thing we are going to have to wait on data for is airbags. Airbags are now widely available for motorcyclists, either as an airbag vest or as an airbag suit. The vest triggers when the lanyard is detached from the motorcycle. The airbag suit deploys when it detects a crash via the GPS and accelerometers. If you watch motorcycle racing, you'll see the racers' motorcycle gear puff up in the upper body. It is subtle, but it is there. I can see how this makes motorcycling a step safer. It just has a steep price tag.

By now you should be seeing how good understanding of the crash data and the technology available to you is putting the odds back in our favor.

The advantages of being Marvel's Ironman

Sadly, there is not nearly enough data on how much gear riders wear and the differences gear makes, but there is some. My own research has consisted of interviewing a trauma surgeon and talking to police officers, firefighters, and paramedics. Weather is the main factor in who wears gear and who doesn't. The hotter it is, the less gear riders wear. Naturally, hotter climates face worse injuries as a result. Setting that aside, if riders are geared up, they will face less serious injuries. The only study that shows the benefits of wearing gear with crash stats was done by Professor Rebecca Ivers in Australia. Several of the first responders I have talked to agree that gear makes a difference. However, they were quick to point out that it is not a guarantee. No amount of safety gear protects the human body from hitting a stationary object at a high speed.

Visibility can play a key role in your safety. A New Zealand study showed that a brightly coloured helmet keeps you visible. A black helmet just can't compare because it does not catch the attention of other drivers. You could go even further by wearing high-vis clothing every time you ride. Some riders do. These can be some of the safest riders out there. They take it seriously. The riders that take it seriously generally do a lot of other things to keep safe, too. Motorcycle riders do like to look good. Wearing the brightest colours isn't always cool. Black-on-black looks sleek, but drivers can't see you. If they can't see you, they can't hit you, right?!

Even if you do everything right

Even if we are perfect riders following all the rules, we can still crash. Crashing is still the biggest fear of riders and mothers everywhere. Even tipping over at a standstill can be scary. No one wants a big machine falling on them. At slow speeds, the chances of serious injury are slim. They're even lower if you're geared up, and that is a big factor. You'll wonder why so few riders wear motorcycle gear, and it is mainly because they have not crashed – yet. Riding motorcycles is all good times and sunshine, but everything changes with one crash. So you do want to keep the fear of crashing. It is healthy to have some level of fear. Unbridled optimism and the thought of "it won't happen to me!" is a fantasy. It's good news that crashing is not a big deal most of the time; it's bad news that it happens when you're far too confident and not geared up.

There are several sayings in the motorcycle world: There are bold riders and old riders but no old, bold riders. There are two types of motorcyclists, ones that have crashed and ones that have not crashed yet.

Treat crashing as a reality but don't assume that it will land you in a hospital. So what should you do when it happens? At the moment of the crash, there will be a very brief moment of realization. The next moment you're going to find yourself on the ground, so forget about thinking you can possibly shoulder-roll out of this one. Watch professional motorcycle riders crashing, and you'll see they are along for the "ride." Our brains have a built-in mechanism to protect us from experiencing something awful. Have you ever woken up from a dream where you are about to fall, get hurt, etc.? It is the same thing. The next moment of awareness is you on the ground, either stopped or sliding. You may not even know you're sliding along the ground. This is why it is important to count to ten before trying to get up. My first crash had me sliding along the track, and it was one of the strangest sensations I've experienced. You'll feel like it is not possible and your mind is playing a trick on you. This is why we count to ten and then pat the ground. Imagine trying to get up while sliding along the ground at any speed: you'll go from sliding to tumbling. When reality sets in and you are completely aware you have crashed, do your best not to panic. Remain in control of the situation. If you're seriously hurt, there will be people to help. Remaining in control of the situation is easier said than done, but you'll benefit from it. Let the adrenaline subside. Don't be in a rush to stand up. If you're seriously hurt stay put until help arrives. If you're aware enough to control the situation, get pictures and witnesses. Assign this task to one person – don't yell out what you need. For example, say, "You in the blue shirt, please take pictures. You in the red sweater, please ask if anyone saw anything." By singling out someone, you make them more inclined to respond. This may be really important if the crash is not your fault or it is not clear who was at fault. If you're in a busy area, people will be helping. They may be moving your motorcycle before pictures can be taken. Multiple people will be calling an ambulance. When the ambulance shows up, they will assess you. You can let them take you to the hospital or you can go to your own doctor. Your motorcycle will get towed to the nearest yard. That is the worst of it. Now it's time to recover.

If you're injured or bruised, you will heal up. It'll take time. You will be replaying the moment over and over in your head. You may even have some level of regret, but don't beat yourself up about it. It is a shock to the system to have a serious crash on a motorcycle. Embrace it for what it is, but do not let it control your life. You can control how you are going to handle the recovery. Forward thinking and positive thoughts will allow you to heal faster. There will be low points; let them pass and get back to recovering. If your crash is more serious, listen to the doctors and physiotherapists. They deal with this on a regular basis. Your friends and family will be there for you, even if they didn't approve of you riding a motorcycle. If you are not getting support from them, stick to the ones who are supporting you. It will be really important to have people you can go to physio with. Make friends with whoever else is recovering. Strength in numbers. This may also mean getting a lawyer if your injuries are severe. Talking to a lawyer is free for the initial consultation. They know the system, they know the insurance companies, and they may even know how long your injuries might take to heal. An insurance company may not have your best interest at heart. Getting a fair amount to speed up your recovery and replace lost wages is reasonable. I would not recommend trusting the insurance company without some sort of representation.

So what about your motorcycle? Wherever it ended up, it'll need your attention. With insurance, things can get complicated. First, keep it simple with minor damage. If it is mostly cosmetic damage with a few broken parts, fix it yourself. If the crash was your fault or the insurance company deems it to be your fault, claiming any small amount of damage can affect your insurance rates. Spend the money to fix it yourself. For anything more major, use your insurance. That is what it is there for. You may have to deal with higher insurance rates, but that is the reality of a crash. Best to talk to your insurance provider to understand all the options you have. They'll be asking for your statement and any pictures you have. They may even ask if you have video of the crash. More and more vehicles have dash cams. Some motorcycle riders have helmet cams. Videos do not lie. If you decide to wear a camera, try to avoid putting it on your helmet. It does add weight and creates wind drag. It is the best mounting point, but it comes with extra risk. There are chest mounts and motorcycle mounts that will tell the story, too. If I was commuting to work on my motorcycle, I would use a GoPro Session. It is the same camera I use on the track and special roads on my trips. It is nice to capture moments but not necessary to capture every single moment.

Worth the risk

Plenty of riders know the risk of riding motorcycles. Some have experienced the worst of it and still ride motorcycles. There is something about motorcycles that makes us crave the risk. It's who we are. Every time we get on the motorcycle, we face the risks, but you know what it takes to reduce it. Significantly. This is why I don't rely on just luck. I have had my lucky moments before, but I know I can't rely on them. I don't want to scare you away from riding, but you will fall off your motorcycle. If you want a very good chance of crashing as little as I have (on the streets), take many advanced rider training courses. This is where you can grow as a motorcyclist and if you crash, you should be OK. It is always better to fail at something in a safe environment. Beat the odds, beat the stats, and be smart about riding. Not nearly enough of us are.

Chapter EIGHT

Traffic Laws and Traffic Fines

Even drivers with clean records can lose their licenses when they get a motorcycle. It can be so much easier to do things that are against the law. The problem is that those things don't always feel like they are against the law. So it does require a great deal of discipline to avoid traffic fines. Speeding is the easiest, as all motorcycles move quickly.

Even the small ones (250 cc) can accelerate past traffic with ease. Since motorcycles are very maneuverable, cutting through traffic or cutting vehicles off may seem harmless, but it's not in the eye of the law. You can earn yourself a stack of traffic fines. Motorcycling is costly enough – let's go through how to stay on the good side of the law while still having a lot of fun.

Being street legal

Before you even leave your garage, your motorcycle has to be fit to ride on the road. This means having at least one mirror, signals (front and back), a headlight, taillight, reflectors, and a visible license plate with a light. A brand-new motorcycle from a dealer is 100 per cent street legal. The moment you start changing things, you do run the risk of getting a ticket or fine. If you must remove or change your mirrors, you need at least one to be legal. The signals can be whatever you want them to be, almost. An integrated taillight is a brake light with signals. The signals light up the left or right side of the light. This looks great, but traffic law states that the two signal lights must be separated. Headlights must be white or light yellow. You cannot get fancy with colours. Same with the taillight: it must be red. An aftermarket taillight can flicker or do some other high visibility flashes. Amber lights can be put anywhere on the motorcycle (this is what semi-trucks do). The reflectors are usually the first to go, but removing them does put you offside. Lots of riders eliminate their fender and license plate for a cleaner look. It looks great but unless the license plate is highly visible and has its own light, it won't be allowed. That said, you could change all of this and never get caught. If the police do take issue with your motorcycle, you'll get an inspection ticket. That means you'll have to make the motorcycle legal and show them that you have done so. You may also just get a fine.

Filtering and splitting

Filtering is the act of slowly moving through stopped or slow traffic. Splitting is usually interpreted as rushing between traffic. They're very different. Out on the road, a good general rule is to act as if you are a car or truck. If you wouldn't do it in your car, don't do it on your motorcycle. It is in our nature to find more efficient ways to do things. Getting home faster by squeezing our way through traffic works in most parts of the world but not in most of North America. So do not filter through traffic or lane split. Right now, California is the only place in North America that allows splitting. You can even move to the front of the line at a red light. It is a thing of beauty. It also works very well. Motorcycles can move through traffic easier and therefore get out of the way of traffic sooner. I wish more states and provinces would allow this. Even though it is illegal in most of North America, several riders do it anyway. On hot days in traffic, there might as well be no law at all, with the amount of motorcycles that filter through traffic. This doesn't mean it is OK, but it tells me that riders do not care.

Before I became a motorcycle instructor, I filtered through traffic all the time. Because I could lose my instructor license, I no longer do it. Sad. If you intend to filter (don't split) through traffic, do it in the most respectful way possible. This means only going 15 km/h (10 mph) faster than traffic, and only where you find the most space between vehicles. Be extra vigilant, as other traffic does not expect you to be there. Expect to be cut off. You're in the wrong here so don't get upset. This will still earn you a traffic ticket, but maybe the officer will see that you are being respectful and sweating it out in your motorcycle gear. Or maybe you were flying through traffic – now they are going to write you up with a stack of fines. Be very nice and respectful. If we ever want filtering to be allowed, we as motorcyclists must prove that it benefits the cars and trucks, too.

It is up to you to be fully aware of the laws. Claiming ignorance does not always work but you can try. If you have been driving cars for a long time. You might not even know what the new laws are. When I teach classes and inform students of the various ways to get tickets, quite often a lot of them don't know the new laws. It doesn't mean they're ignorant. It may just mean they forgot, or they are too busy to review it. Review your local laws and, even better, ask about them. Do not be afraid to talk to a cop about common fines for motorcyclists. A short conversation could save you a lot of money.

Speeding

If we were to poll all riders on what tickets they get most, we would hear a lot about speeding. Getting your motorcycle up to speed and well past it is very easy. It also looks like we are going faster, which doesn't help either. When it comes to speed, you'll need to be more careful on your motorcycle than in your car. It might seem like cops unfairly target us, but whatever the truth is, that's the reality we face. If you intend to speed, keep it reasonable. The general rule seems to be that ten over the limit is tolerable. It is completely up to the officer. Some officers will give a ticket for being slightly over the limit; some have a much higher tolerance for speed. So it can be challenging, especially when the flow of traffic is much higher than the speed limit.

If you are going well over the speed limit, then you are signaling to everyone that you don't care. Do not expect any sort of courtesy from anyone. Just because you are going significantly faster (over 30 km/h or 20 mph faster), doesn't mean they need to get out of your way. Traffic does not expect fast moving vehicles, and a speeding motorcycle can be quite a surprise. You can easily scare motorists, so expect the most unexpected reaction. You're a fighter jet buzzing a small village in the mountains. That's what it feels like to be in the car when a motorcycle blows past a car at an insane speed. The point I am trying to make here is to keep it to yourself and that you can't get mad at traffic. If you are going to break the law, expect the worst and make sure your actions really don't affect anyone else. Motorcyclists get a bad rap most of the time. This kind of behavior doesn't help. So pick your spots and get it over with. If you can't control it, give the track a try. I dare you to see how fast you think you are.

Getting and fighting tickets

Now if you do get pulled over, find somewhere safe to do so. Don't just stop. Slow down and acknowledge the police with a wave. If you pull over somewhere safe the officer has less to worry about. This will be your first step in getting out of this ticket. Before you engage with the officer, put yourself in their boots. They see you as doing something reckless, and they may not understand why anyone rides a motorcycle at all. They see the worst of the worst. So what you did is just a moment away from doom for you and a lot of paperwork for them. Their job is to uphold the law, whatever the law is. Even if they disagree with it, they still have to enforce it. So do not be surprised if they issue you a big fine for doing something you feel was not that bad. They just do not see that way. You might get the cop that really wants to do their job really well. In the moment you are pulled over, decide whether you want to try to get out of it or fight your way out of it in court. If you are good with words and making friends, try your best to win them over. This might mean admitting that what you were doing was risky. The more you say, the more it can be used against you. If you are upset about the whole thing, keep it check. Being angry, short, ignorant, etc. is just going to get you the ticket and maybe a couple extra ones for being such a jerk. They have the badge, the gun, and the law on their side. You do whatever they say, even more so if you are riding in another country. Things can go from simple to handcuffed quickly. Be nice. Assault them with kindness. If you are going to fight the ticket no matter what, say as little as possible. The more you speak, the worse it can be for you. More and more police officers have body cams, so everything is recorded. This is good, but it is also catching more and more people in lies. Take as many notes as you can so you remember all the details. Ask for the ticket and fight it in court. You may have better odds with a judge than with a cop. There is also the option of getting the ticket and writing a letter for a lesser fine. If you're guilty, you can pay the fine and move on with life. Your time may be worth more.

Thankfully, I have had limited interactions with police. In the times that I have, some luck and being nice (I'm Canadian) have helped immensely. I do like a spirited pace on my motorcycle, so I am at risk constantly, but that doesn't mean I treat the roads like race tracks. If I did, I would not be here today to write this book. My strategy for staying away from tickets is never to speed in cities, towns, and school zones. Not worth it. In the mountain passes, I like to open it up, but I do face higher risk. My self-preservation runs high, so I just can't ride like a maniac for long periods of time. I see the outcome. It ain't pretty.

In the moment the police are behind me with lights flashing, I'll pull over when it is safe to do so. I'll turn the motorcycle off, take the key out of ignition, and place it visibly on my seat. I'll take my helmet off and get my license and registration ready. When the cop approaches, they see that I'm probably not high risk. Remember, they deal with the worst of people on a regular basis. Make this easy for them. You will of course get questioned, and it is up to you on the route you take here. I like being nice—they have the gun. If I get a ticket, I will immediately write a letter to reduce the fine. I'll even add in an explanation of why I should not pay it, but it might mean I have to plead guilty to the charge. If I am really upset about the whole thing, I will fight it in court, but this becomes a time commitment. I'll accept my fate even if that means paying a fine. My time is worth more. I just tell myself it is a tax on having so much fun riding motorcycles.

One of the first times I was pulled over was with a few of my buddies. We saw the lights immediately and pulled over rather quickly. The officer stepped out of the car and commented how surprised he was that we stopped. I guess he encounters a lot of people who try to run away. The officer checked out the paperwork and saw that we were all fully geared up. He remarked on our speed but since we were geared up, insured, and our bikes were legal, we just received a verbal warning. One of the strangest tickets I received was from a fisheries officer in the desert. It was confusing getting a ticket from a fisheries officer, especially in the desert. As we were riding, traffic was moving over to the shoulder to let us by. This is a really nice gesture, so it is easy to take people up on it. The fisheries officer was in the oncoming lane when he saw us running people off the road. That is how he saw it. He was completely mistaken, but he had the gun and the badge, so we took the ticket. The frustrating part is that we had to pay it. We were not allowed to pass a car in that area, even if they had pulled over to let us. It was a small fine, so the cost to pay it was less than to fight it.

Radar detectors can save you from speeding tickets, but they are no guarantee. They can easily be your first step in getting that ticket — by the time they pick up the radar, it might be too late. I have never owned one myself, but I have benefitted from them. Several riders I know will not ride without them. So if I am riding with them, I make sure they are out front. If they get a warning it is usually followed by a slow-down and a tap on the head. You can also warn other riders around you with a hand tap on your helmet. It is a universal signal for "cops nearby, slow down." If the police officer has active radar running, meaning their radar gun is sending out constant signals, the radar detector might be able to pick it up early and warn you. If the cop is only using it when he thinks a vehicle is speeding, then you will not get a warning. Laser detectors or jammers don't always work, either. They operate on frequencies, and if you do not have the right one, it will not detect the radar. The phrase "you get what you pay for" applies here, too. A $100 radar detector isn't worth it. It is only good for detecting automatic doors at stores. You have to spend some good money on some of the higher-end models like Valentine or Escort. If you have a big budget, get the Stinger. None of these are perfect, so you cannot speed worry-free.

Where I live, excessive speeding can get your motorcycle impounded. Getting caught going over 40 km/h (25 mph) over the speed limit will leave you on the side of the road with no motorcycle and a heap of fines. In Australia they are even more aggressive against speeding, as they will crush your motorcycle if you are caught going more than 50 km/h (31 mph) above the speed limit. It is pretty harsh. It's the trend to see more enforcement in speeding. It doesn't always add up to fewer crashes, but I see the merit in it. If you want to ride motorcycles fast, you face increased risk to yourself and your wallet is going to get raided. You may even lose your license. I do encourage everyone to fight their tickets, but pick your battles. If you deem it worth to fight, consider finding a lawyer or retired traffic cop. You can hire them, and they might save you a lot of money. They may even keep you from losing your license. On the court date, you might even be so lucky as to have the officer not show up. That would be an automatic win for you. Do not count on it, though.

Chapter NINE

Lane Positioning

Lane positioning is a never-ending debate. This chapter can be a short one with one simple statement: If you always arrive home safely, your lane positioning is correct. Choosing the right lane position is an art not a science. You'll have to pick the proper position in any situation you're in, and the situation changes as you ride down the road. Let's make this simple:

-The left side of the lane is lane position one
-The middle of the land is lane position two.
-The right side of the lane is lane position three.

- If you live in Australia, Hong Kong, the United Kingdom or any of those "reversed" countries, reverse the order.

Most of the time, lane position one is the one you want. Lane position one may feel exposed and vulnerable, but this is where you get respect. Traffic is not going to respect you riding along the sidewalk or off to the side. Stay visible and in the left side of your lane. Other traffic does not want to run you over, and lane position one means you are serious about your safety and demand respect. Lane position two and three are not far away, and you always have options while riding down the road. Remember you are the most maneuverable vehicle on the road, so you have the greatest chance to get out of that dangerous situation.

Safety and distance

Always maintain the greatest amount of distance from your greatest threat. There are always threats to your safety, so prioritize them. This may mean you still have to ride close to something you don't want to be close to. If that is the lesser threat, so be it. Think about this for a moment. Think about how many variables can change as you ride. It can be overwhelming, but you'll be fine as long as you remain 100 per cent focused on riding.

Let's say you are riding alongside traffic and on the other side is a concrete barrier. I'll choose to ride closer to the concrete barrier, as I know that the barrier is not going to blindly change lanes into me. I have now put the greatest distance between me and my potential threat. If that car changes lanes, I will have some reaction time, hopefully enough to speed up or slow down out of the way. As you know, everything else out there has the right of weight compared to you.

What about busier situations? If you are riding on busy interstates and cars are on either side of you, you may have to ride in the middle of the lane and stay hyper vigilant. If I am riding in a lane that has a sidewalk, I will stay away from it. Sidewalks have driveways, so cars could be entering traffic. You just don't get respected or seen (as well) riding right near the sidewalk. If you ride a bicycle, you know what I mean. Traffic will respect you riding in the left side of the lane, position one.

The most dangerous place

Intersections have the greatest chance to hurt you and ruin your love of riding motorcycles. Even with the rules and everyone following the rules, this is where chaos ensues. We all know people do not always follow the rules of the road. It could be sheer stupidity (most of the time) or drivers taking chances. When riding your motorcycle through an intersection, you should always exercise greater caution compared to driving your car. As you approach the intersection, ease off the throttle. This minimal precaution will give you a moment longer to scan the intersection and see if it is safe. Never ever rush an intersection. This means never rushing to make the light or catch up to your rider buddy. Traffic has a hard time judging the speed of a motorcycle. If you are accelerating, they won't know it. The best practice is to ride a little slower through the intersection, covering your brakes and preparing for the unexpected.

The single most common accident in an intersection is the motorcyclist hitting the vehicle turning in front of them. Imagine yourself riding straight through an intersection. You have the right of way, and it is relatively quiet. There is a car on the other side of the intersection, waiting. They have their left turn signal on, and they are waiting for their moment to cross oncoming traffic. You acknowledge this vehicle, and it appears the driver sees you. You feel confident to continue on through. Next moment the left-turning car is in front of you and you have no time to stop or go around. Smash. You become airborne. You hit the ground and you're hurt. This is far too common an occurrence. Never ever assume the oncoming traffic sees you. You can reduce your risk by slowing down (ease off the throttle) and moving away from the vehicle that might turn in front of you. Move to lane position three or move to the next lane over, but put space between you and that vehicle. This will give you a much greater chance of getting through the intersection safely. I can't recommend this enough. If I were to ask all the students I've trained what hurt them or scared them the most, it would be this scenario. So please never ever rush or become complacent riding through intersections.

The danger never ends with intersections. There are endless situations that can hurt you. So let's use some tools to identify risks and mitigate them. As you approach an intersection, look for the crosswalk signals. Does it show that it's safe to walk, is it warning pedestrians to stop walking, or is it telling them not to walk? This is a great indicator on when the light will change. If the pedestrians are walking across, you still have time to make it through the intersection. If the crosswalks are empty and the signal shows no crossing, you know that light will change soon. My favourite is the countdown timer: it shows how long the pedestrians have to walk across. When this timer runs out, it usually means the light will change. Use this information for good, not evil. If the timer shows five seconds left, then do not rush the intersection to make the light. Chances are someone else is doing the same thing. We all want to get to where we are going in the shortest amount of time. Don't rush the intersection. Better yet, take a route that has fewer intersections. You'll see the most accidents (all vehicles) in intersections. Avoid them and enjoy a safer ride.

The danger isn't just in the intersection. It is surrounding it as well. Let's say you're riding down the street and the light changes to yellow and you slow down quicker than you thought. The car behind you thought you were going to go through the light or misjudged your stopping distance and rear-ends you. This is another common occurrence when stopping, especially when it is a quicker stop. High-risk moments are those when you are the first to a red light, at merge lanes, and in the unexpected dramatic slowdowns – think the cliché kid running into the street chasing a ball. In these situations, the greatest danger is now behind you. Check your mirrors and be sure traffic behind you is indeed stopping. If you set up your stop correctly, you have options. Stopping to the left or right of the lane is a safe idea. You are easier to avoid, and you can get out of the way more easily. Stopping in the center of the lane doesn't give you many options, especially if there is a stopped vehicle in front of you. If know you are going to get rear-ended, it is go time. Move forward, move left or right, or run away from your motorcycle. Sometimes, all that is needed is you moving forward a few extra feet. It is easy to become complacent when stopped. A quick search on YouTube will give you plenty of examples of riders getting rear-ended. You will see that most of them have some time to get out of the way.

Intersections are a necessary evil of riding motorcycles. I prefer riding outside city limits, and the lack of intersections is one reason. But we all have to ride through them. Commuting on a motorcycle will mean you'll be riding through plenty of them. Always stay vigilant, trust no vehicle, and take it easy. We all have a few extra minutes to arrive safely. The saved time rushing intersections will never be worth the risk of serious injury.

The open road

The highways are what we think of when we ride. Just the open road and us cruising it. There's a lot less to worry about on highways, but we are riding at a higher speed. Lane positioning is still very important. You'll be on multilane highways, and lane position one is still where you want to be. Lane position three works only if there is a safety space beside you. If the lane you are riding beside is full of traffic, choose the other side. Remember, that concrete barrier (or something else) is much more predictable than traffic.

Since we tend to overreact when forced to make a quick decision, the consequences could be higher on a highway. Always give yourself the largest safety margin you can. This includes stopping distance. You won't always be able to out-brake other vehicles. Pick a lane position that offers the greatest escape route for getting out of the way and stopping. Imagine riding down a highway and there is sudden slowdown in traffic. You know you can stop but can traffic behind you stop? You may have to take your escape route (shoulder) immediately.

Oncoming traffic on quieter highways can be a concern, too. As you enter corners, you may find oncoming traffic cutting the corner. You may have half of a vehicle in your lane. This is another reason why we enter corners from the far side, away from oncoming traffic. You just don't know what is coming around that corner. If the highway becomes busier with traffic on the side of the road. There may be no safe lane position, and that means you need to slow down. A slower speed can be the best defense.

Urban versus rural

We're just scratching the surface of riding a motorcycle with proper lane positioning. I hope you're seeing the strategy involved when choosing a lane to ride in. You'll always be able to reduce your risk significantly choosing the correct lane position. If your visibility is blocked by various vehicles and objects, you may have to slow down. An urban environment will challenge you the most with proper lane positioning. There are more intersections, people, cars, poles, etc. That's not to say it is impossible to stay safe when commuting to work. You'll need to have a good and disciplined approach to your ride to work or through a cityscape. Resist the urge to aggressively move through traffic. It is just too easy for things to change quickly, forcing a decision you may not be able to make. The rural environment does make lane positioning a heck of a lot easier to deal with. Be careful with open road, as the speed quickly becomes the dominating factor. If your speed exceeds the limits and flow of traffic, you've become the greatest risk to yourself. Proper lane positions will not save you from your own speed.

Rural is the safer place to ride at respectable speeds. However, the urban environment can be safe, too. Do not ever feel helpless or trapped in your riding position. You do have options. It'll take time to learn proper lane positioning. Have discussions with your rider buddies. They may be highly opinionated, but a good discussion does well to educate everyone.

Chapter TEN

One motorcycle is never enough

At this point, you probably already know what you want to ride – or you're more confused than ever. When I teach people how to ride, it is mainly for the street. More and more people are becoming riders every year, and it shows in the stats. It is still a small percentage of the population in North

America, so rest assured that you are part of an exclusive club.

Never has there been a better time to learn how to ride motorcycles. There are so many good bikes for you to buy that it will be hard to choose. Almost all the manufacturers have smaller, lower-cc motorcycles to choose from. So how do you choose? You could skip this entire chapter by following this one simple rule: Buy something that is easy to manage (weight), is relatively new (two to four years old), and has a smaller engine (less than 600cc). This kind of motorcycle will give you the seat time you need to get the initial learning or rust out of the way. When you want to move on, it will be an easy sell. The biggest market to sell a motorcycle in is the new-rider market but you need a new-rider friendly bike to sell.

Needs versus wants versus your life

The very reason you learned might have been the motorcycle you saw. It had the latest tech, the sex appeal, and pure awesomeness. That usually comes with big power, a big price tag, and big risk. Never buy your dream bike as your first bike unless it is smaller than 600ccs. Do you really want to ride your dream bike into the ditch? It is easier to do than you think. I have no shortage of new riders buying the latest, greatest motorcycle. It even makes me jealous, but a little part of me dies inside when they crash it. Respect these big machines and learn the basics on something smaller. There is no shame or embarrassment in that, but it is, of course, your life. You certainly can buy a big bike or your dream bike right away. It just means you have to be very careful at the beginning, and the learning curve is steep. You'll look like a new rider as those bigger bikes do take skill to ride smoothly.

I love the lower-cc motorcycles, as they are so easy and fun to ride. I used to dismiss them as a starter bike, but when the Yamaha R3 (sport bike) came out, that all changed. Same can be said for the Honda Rebel 300 (cruiser) and the BMW GSA300 (adventure). These are the right tool for the job of learning or getting excited about riding again. They have the latest tech like ABS and LED lighting. The designs do not look like an entry-level motorcycle either. I love these smaller motorcycles so much because they are so easy to ride. They still accelerate faster than most cars and are just fine on the highway at 130 km/h (81mph). For example, I was on an overnight ride with my two other riders. They had bigger bikes, and I was on a Kawasaki Ninja 400. I was able to keep up and even lead. The motorcycle didn't feel strained or under-powered. Where it was lacking was acceleration and some comfort. Small bikes can do 70 to 90 per cent of what bigger bikes can do.

A new, entry-level motorcycle costs around $5,000 and even less for used. This is a very affordable start. The most ideal motorcycle to buy for any new rider is the motorcycle that is two to four years old with about 5,000 km (3,000miles) on the odometer. It should have had its first service done, and all you need to do is insure it, gas it, and go. If the allure of a new motorcycle is too much and you buy one, it is exciting. You're the first to ride it but you do have to pay the dealer fees and setup. It is extra money that doesn't have to be spent buying lightly used.

Sport bikes, naked sport bikes, and sport touring

The motorcycle that looks fast parked. They come from the race track and get a set of headlights and signals to make them street legal. It can be a short trip from a race-ready motorcycle to a street-ready one. If you are strongly considering something sporty, you're in for quite the ride.

Sport bikes are incredible at acceleration, cornering, and speed. What they are not is comfortable. This is the big trade-off in sport and performance. It has also contributed to falling sales in sport bikes. This is changing; they are making them more comfortable. The Yamaha FZ07, FZ09, and MT10 are great sport bikes that are comfortable to ride. Even Ducati makes some comfortable sport bikes like the Monster and the SuperSport. Sport touring is a nice blend of both worlds. The Ninja 1000SX marries performance and comfort beautifully. This segment of sport bikes has been growing steadily and is one of my favourites. If you decide to ride sport bikes, it is hard to be disciplined on them. They love to go fast. At higher speeds they just feel comfortable, which leads to a false sense of security. If you ride them slow, it just becomes no fun. Imagine driving a Ferrari around a parking lot... Mamma mia!

Sport bikes come in all sizes – from the monster 1400 cc right down to 125 cc. It can be tough to choose what is right for you. A small 250 cc on a sport bike is capable of doing everything on the street, highways included. At 600 cc and above, it gets ridiculous. In a fun and exciting way, it can destroy your driving record. It may also bring out a thrill-seeking monster in you. These motorcycles are highly engineered and have some of the most advanced technology. You are getting a supercar level of performance for 5 to 10 per cent of the price. You just can't beat that value, but it does come at the cost of a massive increase in risk. Be careful of the person you become when riding sport bikes.

If you are smart and like many other smart riders, start smaller with sport bikes and work your way up. By working your way up, I mean taking advanced rider training courses and doing track days. Do not view these as an unnecessary risk or dangerous. They are key to learning what your sport bike is capable of. Most sport bike riders do not know the capabilities of their own motorcycles. As mentioned in the stats chapter, they can be four times more dangerous than any other type of motorcycle.

Everyone should ride one to see what it is about. I've had students hate the look and idea of them but love to ride them. Hopefully the motorcycle training program you took had a sport bike for you to try. If not, take advantage of a demo day at a dealer. More and more I see motorcycles that blend the different categories in an attempt to appeal to the broadest audience. Fair warning, these motorcycles are a serious threat to your driving record.

Cruisers, standards, and other motorcycles with round headlights

When we think of motorcycles, it's usually these ones that come to mind. It's the motorcycle your dad owned, the bad guy from the blockbuster movie, or the hipster with a man bun. It's the motorcycle with a round headlight and an upright or relaxed riding position. My first impression of cruisers came from my motorcycle course on a small Honda Rebel 250. Imagine what it would be like to ride your couch down the road – that's what a cruiser is. It is a great, relaxed way to see the country you live in. Cruise those big long roads taking in the scenery. So they are comfortable for very long rides. You'll have lots of storage options too. Where they can be weak is performance and weight. They are cumbersome to move around at slower speeds. It can also feel under-powered given the large engines they have. They are meant to cruise, so if you are looking for higher performance in a cruiser, check out the Ducati Diavel. Just like sport bikes, there are blends in performance and cruising.

Cruisers typically have bigger engines, so they quickly go from a small 250 cc engine to 800 cc and higher. The Honda Rebel 300, Kawasaki Vulcan S, and the Harley-Davidson Street 500 & 750 are good choices. This is a very different power compared to sport bikes. You'll have lots of power at lower speeds, making it easier to ride at legal speed limits. Your foot pegs or floorboards have lower clearance than all other motorcycles. If you take a corner too sharply, they'll scrape. These motorcycles are good at cornering, but don't get too spirited about it. Doing so can start a spark show that precedes a crash. These motorcycles can get as much technology as sport bikes, but they are slower to embrace them. It is just not needed, unless you are buying a top-of-the-line touring cruiser.

Outside cruisers, you have a myriad of other choices. Scramblers, standards, and choppers. Scramblers and standards are the original motorcycles. They're where it all began. They're also what is popular right now. At the time I am writing this book, a motorcycle with a round headlight and a comfortable seating position is all the rage. With good reason. It satisfies the need of any motorcyclist. Comfortable to ride, good power, good storage options. It will only be weak in wind protection. You will get beat up by the wind. It will not be like a boxing fight, but at the end of a long ride, you'll feel it. You'll also get used to it, too.

I understand why I see mostly these types of motorcycles on the road. At the same time, they also force you to be disciplined. They really do ride well. I do see myself on one in the future. They will not inspire aggressive riding the way sport bikes do. Cruisers and standards will also retain their value better, as they are more popular.

Adventure and offroad motorcycles

This is the motorcycle that can do it all, almost. You like the idea of riding in the street, but you like the dirt riding, too. This is what the aptly named adventure motorcycle is made for. Riding on the highway and transitioning to the dirt trails comes easily to these motorcycles. If I were to choose their closest relation, it would be dirt bikes. You can consider them a dirt bike with street-capable performance. You'll sit upright, up high, and take on whatever the world throws at you. If a zombie apocalypse happens, this is the motorcycle you will need to have gassed up and ready to go.

Even the smallest adventure motorcycles are tall, and if you're not tall enough, it'll be tougher to ride. They need to be this tall, so they have the clearance to ride over rocks, jump fallen trees, and cruise through creeks. Don't be too intimidated by this, as when you sit on it, your weight should lower it by a few inches. Just like everything else, it is good to start smaller. Smaller means smaller engine. The Versys 300, BMW GSA300, and the KLR650 are all good choices. They'll come in the under $10,000 price category and if they fall, they are easy to pick up. Being easy to pick up is key, as you have to be able to pick it up in tough conditions. The seating position is upright, which makes it easy to ride. Easier than riding a sport bike and easier than riding a cruiser, more and more motorcycles of all types are being designed with an upright seating position. So once you're riding it, you'll find it is a breeze to ride. Even if this style of motorcycle is not your thing, it'll be the easiest to learn the basics on.

Once you go up in size, features, and weight, price goes up as well. It's all worthwhile as long you keep it under 1,000 ccs. This mid-range category is the sweet spot for everything. Ride from your house to your favorite trails or take it on a world adventure. If you delve deeper into adventure riding, you'll find most of the adventure riders are in the mid-range size. They deliver on almost anything you can throw at them.

If you venture into the large adventure bike category, welcome. These are the flagship machines of the big adventure brands such as BMW and KTM. Ewan McGregor and Charley Boorman showed this in riding their BMW GSA1200s all over the world in *Long Way Round* and *Long Way Down*. These motorcycles will require a good level of skill in both street and the dirt. If you're of shorter stature, you'll need a ladder to climb them. I'm over six feet, and even my feet are not flat on the ground. Since they are flagship motorcycles, expect them to exceed the $20,000 mark with ease.

The perfect motorcycle

There will never be a motorcycle that can do it all. The closest you'll get is a motorcycle that can do most things well. Even then, you'll find limitations. The big factors are price, size, capabilities, and comfort. When I get into discussions on what motorcycle to buy, it's easy to figure out the main reason you want a certain motorcycle, but the secondary reason is usually the problem. It goes something like this. I want a sport bike, but I want all-day comfort. I want an adventure motorcycle, but I want to ride rough trails.

I want a cruiser to see the country on, but it's too heavy. We can't have the best of both worlds with motorcycles. You'll need to get the motorcycle you love the most that does what you want it to. You might have to get a second motorcycle for the secondary reason. That said, I don't like the logistics of owning several motorcycles. Too much insurance, maintenance, and space. I had to start a motorcycle school to justify it. That said, I personally love sport bikes. So I own a Ducati SuperSport S, which is a sport bike that is comfortable enough to ride. My second bike of choice is more of an adventure motorcycle like the BMW GSA300. Two different worlds accomplishing everything I need. This is part of the enjoyment of motorcycles – finding and discovering what you love to ride. At the same time, your riding style may change. It'll be tough to marry one motorcycle. Be monogamous with your spouse and a swingin' party animal with motorcycles.

When you do buy a motorcycle, it is tough to judge if it is the right one for you. We all want to make the right decision, but it takes several rides and sometimes even a motorcycle trip to know if we have the right one. Even then, you might find your needs and desires changing and evolving. It is much easier to be satisfied with the car you drive. Motorcycles offer a much more immersive experience. Each motorcycle has its own personality. Enjoy it all.

Chapter ELEVEN

Dirt Bikes

Dirt bikes have their own community much like street riding and racing do. A lot of dirt riders just stay in the dirt and never ride on the street. When a dirt rider goes from the dirt to the street, they make excellent riders. The limited traction in the dirt is part of the fun. The motorcycle will move around a lot, always trying to find traction on whatever it can grip. Your riding is done on trails in some very remote areas. You'll be exploring and enjoying the scenery that very few people see. If you miss it, it's because you are absolutely focused on getting your dirt bike through the trail you're on. The dirt bikes you can choose range from small and lightweight to big and powerful. A small entry-level dirt bike like a Yamaha TTR 125 will cost you about $1,000 used. A larger, more capable dirt bike can cost between $4,000 and $12,000.

A whole new world

A dirt bike can go anywhere you are willing to ride it. Just be aware that you do have to ride out. So go explore and see where you can get yourself. Best to go with a buddy, as you may need help if any problems arise. Most dirt bikes are dirt-only, meaning you can only ride it on dirt roads. It will not have the signals and lights required to be street legal. There are dirt bikes that are street legal. This can make riding to the trails easy. Your other option is to get a truck or trailer to haul your dirt bike around. Street riding offers a smooth experience, but dirt biking will throw you around a lot and you will be muscling your dirt bike through some tough paths. Prepare yourself for a good workout. Depending on where you live, you're going to explore some very beautiful areas. You'll even find decks and patios in the middle of nowhere. So bring a lunch and enjoy it with your riding buddies.

Your basic riding skills are enough to teach you how to ride in the dirt, but choose the easier paths. Much like you would do if you go skiing, choose the green runs. There are also dirt courses for you to take and plenty of YouTube videos for you to watch. The limited traction will feel strange and you should quickly learn that not being on the throttle makes things worse. Your dirt bike needs the constant throttle, as that brings the stability. It's been said since people started riding in the dirt: when in doubt, throttle out!

If you've been riding on the street, you might be leaning into corners. This is an absolute no on the dirt. Leaning is good when you have traction; when you don't, leaning is asking for trouble. The rules for street and dirt riding are drastically different, and this is one of the biggest rules. It is a law of physics, so no getting by this one. This means that you must stay completely upright while the motorcycle is leaning. Your body is straight up like you're sitting in a chair, and the motorcycle is at an angle. The bike may move around, but your body weight holds the centre of gravity steady. The bike can move around and do what it has to do. The bike might be doing all sorts of movements, but it should keep you on it.

You will crash more riding in the dirt. This may sound scary, but you'll be going at lower speeds so most of the time your falls will be minor. Most injuries in the dirt are lower body so do not skimp on the gear. Motocross boots are some of the most rigid and tough. It is equivalent to a cast for a broken leg. It doesn't mean you can skip the upper-body gear, as there are some gnarly rocks, branches, and drop offs you will not want any part of. Full gear for dirt riding. Wear your street gear if you do not have the dirt gear. You're just getting started, so there's no need to fully commit just yet. The great dirt riders wear fairly minimal gear, but they had to crash their way to their skill level. Don't think you are better than you really are. That is Riding 101.

Picking the right bike

Start small for your first dirt bike. You'll have a much easier time handling it, learning it, and picking it up. The moment you get on the trails you'll be focused on staying on your bike. The power will not be of concern. You'll find that dirt bikes can be expensive. Considering how simple they are, they should be a better deal. It comes down to supply and demand. Dirt bikes are popular, and the price point is low enough that most people can afford it. So your small dirt bike will hold its value and be an easy sell when it is time to move up.

On the trails, you'll have to be aware of your fuel range on smaller dirt bikes. The seat will be smaller so the comfort will not be there. No dirt bike is meant to be comfortable. You'll be standing on the pegs and getting off the seat more than you think. I started to learn on a Yamaha TTR 125. It is a small bike, and I am a big guy. It looks ridiculous, but I was having serious fun. I made lots of mistakes, but it was easy to correct and falling wasn't a real concern. If you do not want to go this small, you can do what I did and take a course where the motorcycle is provided. Get the basics learned and buy something bigger.

When you go to a bigger motorcycle, you'll get the power and options you were missing. That comes with a bigger price, a little more comfort, added weight, and good gas range. If you can't pick this motorcycle up yourself, you probably shouldn't buy it. Bigger dirt bike engines offer a lot of power down low. This is why you see videos of people going up trees and through fences. It is a lot of power, right away. The foundation you'll build from the smaller dirt bikes will benefit you well here.

Racing your dirt bike through the air

The world of motocross marries dirt riding with ridiculous jumps. This is not for the faint of heart or the person who does not want to fall. If you can handle the risk, then you will be treated to a thrill even beyond racing on the street. You'll be managing your traction and then managing your airtime as you ride the course. Depending on how you ride the jumps, you'll either land beautifully or (in most cases) crash spectacularly. This is definitely a higher level of dirt riding, requiring some high-end equipment.

If riding your motorcycle through the air is a little much for you, then you can also consider flat tracking. This is the NASCAR of dirt riding and has been a spectator sport since the early 1900s. Most of it is done in an oval, which will require you to slide out the rear tire and drift. You'll keep the throttle on, as sliding the rear tire helps the motorcycle to steer. This should sound ridiculous to you. It is, but the rules of riding are all reversed in the dirt. Learning these skills is hard, whether you know everything or nothing about how to ride. The real beauty of this type of riding is being comfortable with the rear tire sliding. A little is normal and we all should be OK with that. In all types of riding, we will experience limited traction at some point.

Both motocross and flat tracking are exciting and tough to learn. You'll get the best experience taking a course. Find the course that provides everything. This may mean you have to travel, but it is well worth it and still cheaper than buying all the gear and crashing your way to the desired skill level. My entry in the world of limited traction was with American Supercamp. I took a flight from Vancouver to Los Angeles to take their two day course that provides everything. I did not crash very much the first time I took it, and the skills I learned changed my street riding forever. This is when I learned why the fastest and safest street riders are dirt riders as well.

Dirt bike riders make the best street riders

I started riding motorcycles, and years later I learned about riding in the dirt. The limited traction and the way you handle it directly benefits your street riding. On the street we expect traction and when we lose it, we don't know what to do. Dirt bikers know what to do. If dirt riding is not your thing, consider taking a course that provides everything you need. You'll acquire skills that will help you stay safe on the street. In the last ten years of motorcycling, ABS, rider education, and innovations in safety gear have made motorcycling safer. If every rider took a dirt-riding course, it would have the same benefits. Dirt riders really do make excellent street riders.

Chapter TWELVE

Commuting

Cities are getting busier and busier, and the road infrastructure just can't handle it. We've all been frustrated sitting in rush-hour traffic. A lot of people get into riding so they can commute to work faster and enjoy it a little more.

You'll also be automatically much cooler showing up to work carrying a helmet. I am not one of these people, as my home city of Vancouver has rather wet weather and doesn't allow lane filtering. It is more dangerous riding in the city and I just don't enjoy riding city roads. That's just me. I still see a lot of motorcycles commuting to work, so it works for many. It can also mean a faster way to work. So how much better is riding a motorcycle to work?

Choose the right bike for the urban jungle

Go for something lighter and upright for your commute. A full-on sport bike or full-sized cruiser is not going to make your commute much better. Sport bikes want to go, go, go, and their riding position is not comfortable. Cruisers are too heavy and require too much work to balance at slow speeds. It'll be a workout getting these bikes to and from work. What you want is a dirt bike with street tires, a dual sport, a naked upright, or even a scrambler. There are so many choices out there. So stick to this mantra: If it's light and upright, it's right. For example, the Honda CB300R is 330 lb. wet weight (really good), fully upright, good on gas, and cheap on insurance. Something like this is going to make your commute fun. These motorcycles make so much sense because they can get around traffic. You are going to switch lanes at slow speeds, move slowly through stop-n-go traffic, and squeeze through tight spaces. Best of all, small and nimble motorcycles are cheap to operate. In some cases, it's cheaper than buying a monthly transit pass, especially if your city has a transit system with multiple payment levels.

The dos and don'ts of commuting

Use those high-occupancy vehicle (HOV) lanes. These are reserved for multiple-occupancy vehicles, electric vehicles, and motorcycles. Not only will you avoid waiting in traffic, but they also are safer as well. Traffic uses them less, so there should be less traffic switching in and out of the lane. Use caution if traffic is stopped and the HOV lane is moving. The speed variance can prompt unsafe lane changes. Always expect some car to move into the HOV lane at any time. This is a good moment to use the lane position farthest away from the slow (or stopped) traffic.

Do not split or filter your way through heavy traffic. Remember, lane filtering is gently moving through traffic while it is stopped or moving slowly. This means going slightly faster than the traffic. Lane splitting can be interpreted as you are flying through traffic with reckless abandon and no care for your life. While most of the world allows lane filtering, North America does not like it. Only the state of California allows it. So unless you're there, don't do it. That said, I always see riders using the shoulder or riding through traffic. You'll risk getting a stack of traffic tickets from the police officer. Traffic doesn't expect it, and you will surprise drivers. Since traffic does not expect it, there is risk to you. Some drivers all of a sudden become traffic communists (everyone should wait equally!) when they see a motorcycle filtering through traffic and getting home before them. Until it becomes legal where you live, don't do it. And if you are going to do it anyway, be safe about it. Go slowly alongside of stopped (or slow) traffic. Show traffic absolute respect and hope the officer who stops you just gives you a warning. One final warning about riding the shoulder: it is full of sharp objects that can cause a flat tire.

Do take fewer intersections on your way to work. Intersections are the most dangerous place to ride a motorcycle. You have everything to gain by taking a route to and from work with fewer intersections. The urban environment is a more dangerous place to ride than the open road through the mountains. There are too many vehicles and people, and they're all outside your control. Make your commute to work a little adventure on quieter roads if possible.

Parking your motorcycle for free

Riding to work can also mean you get the best parking, sometimes for free. Look for motorcycle-specific parking. It's worth doing a search in your city to see where motorcycles are allowed to park. If there is nothing available to you, finding the spot will be easy enough. If you're in a parking lot, avoid the parking stalls and look for corners and painted-off areas. Those are places where cars will never park and people will never walk. These spaces are usually OK if it is city lot or a free private lot. In a private paid lot, all vehicles need a ticket. Stay off walking paths and sidewalks. Your motorcycle will get ticketed and towed. If you are going to park up against a building, ensure you are not on a sidewalk. There is a boundary between a public sidewalk and private property. Figure it out and tuck your motorcycle away. Parking your motorcycle for free is a bit of an art. If you find a perfect spot, also respect the people around it. If you have to ride your motorcycle through people walking, don't do it. Get off the bike and push it quietly to where it needs to go. A lot of people are scared of motorcycles and they just assume you'll lose control and run them over.

As far as metered spaces go, pay for them. If you are trying to piggyback off a space that contains a car, park right at the meter. If it's a double-headed meter, it is ambiguous as to which space you are in. If both meters have money, you'll be OK. If you are going to park outside a metered space, make sure it is not close to a stop sign. If it is too close, you can get a ticket – unless you are in San Francisco where parking near a stop sign is OK. Every city has its own rules. A creative motorcyclist can get free parking easily.

When you're done for the day, now you get to ride home. What a perfect end. Or is it? We have all had rough days at work. Riding a motorcycle when excessively stressed from work is not a good idea. You will not be in the right frame of mind for riding. Riding frustrated or angry can lead to many mistakes and even road rage. Even under your normally calm demeanor, getting cut off by another car can cause you to fly into a rage. If you are already upset, the things you might do to the offender could land you in serious trouble. We are not at our best when angry, so take the extra time to calm down and enjoy the ride home. It might be exactly what you need after your tough day. Punching a mirror off a car or kicking a door may feel good at the moment, but all you do is make yet another motorist hate motorcyclists.

Or do all things illegal on a pedal-assist ebikes

Traffic can easily ruin your love of riding if you ride the wrong bike in traffic. Even on something nimble, moving as slowly as cars and trucks can ruin the fun. Enter the pedal-assist ebike. This is your standard bicycle with an electric engine. So it looks like a bicycle and rides like a bicycle but moves with ease anywhere. Even big hills are made easy. You'll feel like a superhero with superhero strength pedaling at 30 km/h (20 mph) with only moderate effort. Faster is possible, but the limits of the electric motor are at about 32 km/h (21 mph). Since it is a bicycle, you can ride on the road, ride through parks, and filter through traffic. Nobody cares, not even the law. So imagine commuting to work with no traffic in front of you at all. The road is yours. That is what it is like to ride a pedal-assist ebike to work. Don't want to stop at a stop sign? No problem: just go through it or cut the corner. Traffic is gridlocked? Filter your way through and get home quicker. I do not recommend blowing stop signs or breaking the laws on your bicycle, but there really is hardly any enforcement. Yet. This will change, as something this good is bound to have rules eventually. More and more people are getting onto bicycles, ebikes, and limited-speed motorcycles. City planning is also ensuring adequate bike lanes are available with new construction. I love my pedal-assist ebike and will happily commute to work on it. It is still two wheels and an engine, so I love it.

The bicycle advocates are far more organized than motorcycle advocates, so they seem to be favoured. They also have a better reputation as being green and friendly. The cost of an ebike can very well be as much as a motorcycle, so you may be turned away from it. If your motorcycle commute is not what you thought it would be, this might be a great option for you. You'll even get health benefits, as you'll be moving your legs. Save the motorcycle for the open roads less travelled – the roads where you can ride with just road in front of you. The choice is yours.

Chapter THIRTEEN

Big Rides, Multi-day Rides, and Touring

Hitting the open road for several days is a vacation like no other. You'll get your time off, it'll clear your mind, and it'll challenge you physically and mentally. The number of variables you'll encounter, planned and unplanned, is part of the excitement. These are the stories you'll remember and tell in the off season. Planning is key. You need to do it, or you need to find someone else who does it and does it well. Be sure to buy the beers if they did the planning.

Bring out the map

So where do you want to go? How much time off do you have? How long can you and your group ride for? First off, find your destination; that's the easy part. It really doesn't even need to be a destination, as that is not what motorcycle trips are all about. Now start picking your stops along the way. Do not get too ambitious, as the longer you ride, the more you'll fatigue. Aim to be off the road by 6:00 p.m. at the latest. The later you go, the harder the next day is. On one ride I did, we left from West Wendover, Nevada, to Zion National Park, Utah. What should have been a reasonable day turned into a 1,000 km (600 mile) day. This is too long on a motorcycle for an enjoyable ride. By the time we found ourselves rolling through the amazing sights and scenery of southern Utah, it was dark out. We couldn't see anything and the risk of animals running in front of us was higher. It was past 10:00 p.m. when we arrived. We were exhausted. In the morning we woke up to this beautiful place, but we could not spend much time enjoying it. We were on the road soon and it felt like we didn't even stop in this beautiful place. Not only that — we were also "hungover" from the long day before. Big motorcycle rides take a lot out of you, so give yourself the evening off to relax. You'll even get to take in the local sights and beauty of the place you're staying.

A good rule is to keep it to about 500 km (300 miles) per day. This gives you the option to arrive earlier or take a few interesting roads along the way. You can ride longer, but it depends on the type of roads you will be riding. Get familiar with the different roads available to you. Interstates are great at shortening your day. Secondary highways are quieter but not too exciting. Twisty roads are where the magic happens, but these do slow your day down immensely. Google Maps is my go-to tool in route planning. I also use motorcycle maps like Butler, which cater to the motorcyclists. These two tools ensure your trip will hit up all the great roads along the way, while keeping good time. You will find that the route you plan is not the route you ride. Timing, road construction, weather, fatigue, forest fires, and other random events force you to change the route. It is more important to know the good roads around you and plan as you go.

So just how big of a motorcycle ride should you take? Three to five days is the easiest, as most people can get that time off. Once it gets closer to a week or longer, you'll have a tough time finding riding buddies who can go with you. It's not that they don't want to, but life is busy. If you find a good riding group that can take a week or longer off, stick with them. They're rare. That said, a three- to five-day ride can be a soul-changing experience. Every year, I make a trip down to northern California with my trusted riding buddies. We trailer our motorcycles down, ride for three days, and trailer them back. It takes five days, and at the end we are exhausted, thrilled, and happy. Longer trips will exceed your physical and mental abilities, so consider a rest day or at the very least a half day. Also watch what you are eating: a few healthy meals may be in order.

Packing fast and light

You have the list of necessities for the ride. Now where do all your clothes go? There are several options for motorcycle luggage, starting with backpacks, tail bags, saddlebags, and even trailers. Keep an eye on the weight of your luggage. You can go past a point where your motorcycle feels sluggish with the amount you are carrying. If you decide to camp while riding, this will double the weight you have to carry.

Backpacks are the simplest and easiest way to go, but they can be tough on your shoulders. The constant bumps and movements will cause unnecessary discomfort with the shoulder straps. I would strongly recommend you avoid backpacks for this reason. We can easily exceed what we need to bring and putting that extra weight on our backs will not make our ride more enjoyable. Use backpacks for quick trips only.

Saddlebags are the most common and can hold a significant amount. They are available as soft bags or hard bags. Soft bags will snap onto the side of your motorcycle and still allow room for a passenger. They do tend to move around, so they take adjusting and can take time to take on and off the bike. Use the rain cover when needed, as most soft saddlebags are not waterproof. I've used soft saddlebags for years because they're cheap and light. What I did grow tired of was constantly adjusting them, making sure the weight was balanced, and having them occasionally rub up against things. Hard bags are available, but they will require a rack. These will add weight to your motorcycle, but they sure do look good. Most of them will keep your luggage dry, too. They are not cheap, but the ability to lock them is a nice feature. They attach easily and come off just as easily. A word of warning: the bags will stick out to the side and we are always not aware of just how far they stick out. They can rub up against another motorcycle or a parked car or catch on something we are maneuvering through. This can cause you to knock things over or fall off yourself.

Tail bags sit on the passenger seat or on a rear rack you get installed. This keeps the weight on top of the motorcycle, and you still can pack quite a bit. I prefer this method, as it requires the least amount of adjusting, it is out of the way, and I do not have to worry about them catching on anything else. It does limit your ability to take a passenger. I've used both hard and soft tail bags, and I prefer soft. The weight savings are worth it and if you use drybags, you'll never have to worry about your stuff getting wet. My motorcycle is equipped with two drybags. One sits on the passenger seat and the other on the rack. I secure them with the provided tie-downs and use ROK straps. If you set these up properly, you'll be able to remove them and attach them just as quickly as hard luggage.

Trailers are for when you need to bring absolutely everything with you and want to camp. There are some very unique trailers out there. The bigger ones will have two wheels side by side. This will affect the handling of your motorcycle significantly, so you'll have to travel slower. If the trailer becomes unstable, it will throw you off the motorcycle. This is very hard to recover from. Some trailers have one wheel, which works great for how the motorcycle works. There is more stability but less storage space. Trailers have their place with riders, but they always make me wonder why you wouldn't just drive a convertible?

You'll have plenty of luggage options for your motorcycle. There will be factory options but plenty of other options, too. Check and see what works for others and try different options that work for you. Keep the emphasis on the weight: try to add as little to the motorcycle as possible. You can always keep items like chain lube and tools with other riders.

Camping versus hotels

After a long ride, there is nothing like setting up your tent and unpacking or getting into an air-conditioned room. Which would you prefer? Both are appealing to the right person, but after spending all day outside, it sure is nice to get out of the sun into a cool room with a shower and a cold beer. If you're going to choose the easiest choice, then it is the hotel.

If you are travelling in the summer months, it is best to book your hotel ahead of time. Everyone else is on vacation and they need rooms, so book ahead to save some stress. The best deals happen when you call the hotel directly. However, Expedia and other travel websites can offer better rates. Once you arrive, park your motorcycle in the main drive, also called the breezeway. Almost all hotels I have stayed at have allowed us to park under this cover for the evening. Ask nicely and park it where it is out of the way of the walking paths. This is the safest place for your motorcycle.

Other pro tips on staying at a hotel include asking for a room on the ground level. Even better, try to park right in front of your room. It's much easier to move all your gear and luggage. Ask for the best places to eat and whether they have any deals for hotel guests. If your motorcycle is a genocide of bugs and insects, the hotel usually has some cleaning rags for you to clean it up. Just ask. I've always found hotels to be very accommodating to motorcyclists. I think it is because most of us go to bed early, tired from the ride. One very memorable hotel was in San Luis Obispo. The Quality Suites Downtown offered nice covered parking, easy-to-access rooms, free beer, and $5 barbeque. The patio was an open space with fire columns to keep you warm. I love surprises like that on motorcycle trips.

Camping during your motorcycle trip offers the same peace and quiet of a motorcycle ride. They do go very well together. The extra luggage, however, does not. You must become Marie Kondo in order to pack efficient enough to fit everything on your motorcycle. Even then, it can easily double the weight of your luggage. It may be worth the savings, as camping is cheap, and if you're creative in your camping spots it can even be free. If you have a motorcycle big enough to accommodate lots of luggage, then you'll be all right. On anything smaller, it can affect the handling of your motorcycle. The quality of sleep might not be the same, either, leaving you tired for the next day's ride. Camping is usually more social, so the chances of chatting up other travelers is better.

AirBnB, hostels, and couch-surfing

On a solo ride, it is just you and the road. It can be a Zen-like or meditative experience. It can also mean being alone with your thoughts all day long, and that could be a scary thought right there. If you crave some social time on your trip, then you have some options. AirBnB, hostels, and couch-surfing are great for the adventurous rider. There are more solo travellers than you think.

AirBnB offers some very unique stays with some very friendly people. AirBnb hosts are usually travelers themselves in between trips. It is very much staying in a stranger's house, but don't let that discourage you. Almost all my AirBnB experiences have been good memories to add to my trip. You book them just like you would a hotel, then you show up and stay — you might even get breakfast. One of my favourite stays was in southern Oregon. I showed up late, and I was tired and hungry. They showed me to my room, and I changed and came downstairs and was offered a beer, dinner, and dessert. Those things are not included usually. We sat outside by the bonfire in the warm summer evening. Dessert was peach pie made from peaches from the hosts' own peach tree. There is no way a hotel could top this experience. It didn't stop there. I slept like a rock, as I usually do on motorcycle trips. Breakfast was included, but it wasn't just any breakfast: waffles made from scratch with sweet potatoes and, yes, it was topped with peaches. The sweet potato mixed into the waffle batter gave the waffles a delectable consistency. I had to ask what the recipe was. To this day, I still make sweet potato waffles. Months later, I received a birthday card from them. I have had many AirBnB stays like this and others were quite minimal. You can arrive late and leave early and barely say two words to the host. They will respect your privacy.

Hostels are not just for college students on small travelling budgets. I've found hostels to cater to all types of people looking for a cheaper place to stay. A lot of hostels now offer private rooms and semi-private rooms. If you are just needing a quick and cheap place to stay, consider this. What I love about hostels is the common rooms and social events. It is your choice on how many people you want to chat to. This where solo travelers go to stay; you'll also see young families and even retired couples. I was surprised to see such a diverse crowd staying in hostels. Hostelling International and the Youth Hostel Association offer the higher-end hostels, but always check reviews to see what is the best in town.

If you are extra adventurous, then you can sleep on someone's couch. Couchsurfing.org has been around since 2003 and now has 14 million members. You can find a couch to sleep on almost anywhere in the world. The site offers a review system for both the host and the traveler, so you can easily separate the good from the bad. Just like AirBnB and hostels, I found the same social vibe. It is a community of travelers made by travelers. One of my couch-surfing stays was actually in a bed, and the host was a die-hard Democrat in northern California, which is very Republican. His friend was a Syrian immigrant, which was a country in turmoil and war at the time. The conversation was very eye-opening that night. These types of stays really enhance the trip.

Riding solo versus with a group

Hitting the road solo offers freedom and the promise of a ride on your schedule, but what about the rolling party that a group motorcycle ride can be? Riding solo means your pace, your stops, and your route. It's also hard to organize a group to go on a long ride, so the ease of just going at it alone is appealing. Solo riding will clear your mind and will be a true vacation from your everyday life. It is a physical and mental challenge. It makes it into a rewarding journey that most vacations just can't offer. You can keep to yourself or engage with the locals. One solo ride north through California, there was this pizza joint I had dinner at. All their pizza crusts were handmade and tossed. I sat there enjoying my IPA beer and watching enormous circles of pizza dough flying through the air. It was probably the liquid courage from IPAs and the buzz from my ride, but I asked if I could learn. The restaurant wasn't busy and being that this was a small town, the answer was, sure! I learned how to pound out the dough evenly and the proper placement on holding it. Then came the toss— well, it is all in the wrist, but it was not as hard as it looked. You'd need to toss at least a hundred pizzas to get any sort of consistency, but for a first try, I was satisfied. I made my own pizza, learned the balance of too many toppings and not enough. In the end, they had fun teaching me and I just had to tip them out. It was one more story (and learned skill) from a motorcycle trip. I rode through there years later hoping for a repeat, but sadly the place was closed. Things change surprisingly fast in small towns.

If you're hotelling on your solo ride, you'll have to eat the entire cost of the room, but rest assured that small towns have the best rates. Always ask for a discount or the managers rate. The decor of the small independent hotels can be charming, and some feel like they are stuck in time. The charm is just enough for one night. Wake up the next morning, find the best coffee shop and roll forward.

Breakdowns riding solo are more problematic, as solving it is entirely up to you. If you're well outside city limits, you'll find more people willing to help. If you planned ahead with a roadside-assistance plan, you'll be sorted out quickly. When riding solo, be sure to bring that tire plug and patch kit and more tools than you think you will need. Crashing is certainly a reality on any motorcycle ride. Riding solo—well, let's hope someone sees you off to the side of the road. If you are riding in a remote area, GPS tracking becomes more of a requirement than a recommendation. With today's technology, there is no reason to go off the grid with no tracking. When dealing with the reality of crashing and being the only one to deal with it, you have to remain calm and focused. It's easier said than done but added stress is not going to get you out of your ordeal. This is part of the solo ride, the absolute loneliness you crave. If you can make it out of this predicament, it'll turn into a great story for years to come.

I know plenty of solo riders, and it is definitely part of their personality. It is not my choice of ride to go on but when I have gone on solo rides, they have been incredibly enjoyable. I just enjoy the group rides more. Group rides are what made motorcycling incredible for me. My first taste of group rides was enough to motivate me to plan them. There are never enough planners, so your rides will be well-attended if you become a good ride planner.

Getting groups together for rides is closely related to herding cats. You have the fence-sitters, the last-minute cancellers, and the "I wanna go but" crowd to deal with. The people that are good for your ride are the ones who are there on the scheduled date and at the scheduled time. Don't put too much faith in anyone. Big rides are a big deal. Even once you have your group ready to go, your scheduled leave time will be delayed and stops will take longer. Your scheduled route will see changes, so try to keep people moving; you're burning daylight. This can sound a little discouraging, but the laughs and fun will be well worth it.

No group ride would be complete without some form of drama. This is a reality, so don't be the one to fan the flames of the drama fire. The expectations of people can be wildly unacceptable. Never take sides and always do what the group prefers. If it does get bad, everyone has their own transportation. They can ride away. Problem solved! Friendships can be made and broken on these rides, so look at the big picture. Sometimes you need to cater to the drama queen long enough to get home.

Some of my best group rides have been the biggest. "ExplOregon" is a ride I have set up a few times, and with twenty-four riders, it was the biggest. We rented three houses on the Oregon coast and did day rides. The day was spent on some of the finest roads in Oregon, and the evenings were spent watching the sunset on the beach. We would take over the local restaurant and every night was a party. All-day riding does tire you out, so they never went too late.

Group rides are worth the effort, but choose wisely who you ride with. Riding long distances requires good skill and discipline. There are plenty of riders who don't take it seriously enough, and they are the ones who end up in the ditch. This can ruin your ride. Choose the riders who take advanced courses, wear full gear, and are nice to be around. You'll have to do a few big rides with other riders, but your riding herd will emerge soon enough. You should still always be prepared to go at it alone. You will definitely help each other out, but always be prepared to ride alone if necessary. Don't be the rider who relies on everyone else to get them through the day.

Riding in other countries and shipping your motorcycle

Backpacking around a country is a great way to experience it. Now imagine it with a motorcycle. You get the best of both worlds now. The logistics of setting this up is daunting. Most just don't do it or start and give up. The hardest part is the amount of money required up front to ship your motorcycle. This is a great deal of trust for something you're attached to. No motorcyclist likes to leave their motorcycle with people they don't know very well. Thankfully, the internet has made this easy. At uship.com, all you have to do is list your shipment and identify where it needs to be picked up and dropped off. Shippers will then bid for your business. Since they are all reviewed, you can pick the ones with the best reputation. This is my chosen method when I ship my motorcycle across the country. You also have the option of air transport. You and your motorcycle can fly to the country you want to ride in. Most airlines have minimal requirements. They'll require a near-empty gas tank, a disconnected battery, and minimal luggage. Your motorcycle should be flown out on a flight before your own. It is not like checked baggage that shows up after the flight. It'll take a day. You will most likely need someone on the other side to clear customs for you. You can do it yourself, but depending on the location and what is required, this is best left to someone who knows the system. Don't waste your precious vacation days. Costs will be expensive. I know what it costs from Canada, and other places seem similar as well. It is safe to say you are on the hook for $1,000 each way, with currency conversion being a factor as well. If that sounds like too much work and money, you have the option of renting. There are several motorcycle rental businesses. Where it might be cost prohibitive is for longer trips. Daily costs with insurance can be between $200 and $300. You are then also on the hook for any damage (however minor). I'd recommend this for shorter trips, and it is the easiest. For longer trips, put the effort in and fly your motorcycle out. If you're committed to this, it will also be a great idea to see what sort of insurance coverage you need. Your current insurance may not cover you in a foreign country. When I rode in Baja, Mexico, all I had to do was signup with a company that caters to motorcycle riders. It was all done online and seemed easier than it should be. Whatever the case, do this well before you go away. The last thing to consider is a GPS tracker, such as a SPOT transponder. This way you can send your family a GPS message that you are OK, they can check on you, and if something goes wrong, they'll get the emergency signal and put someone on it.

Riding abroad is an expensive ordeal — or is it? There are adventure riders out there who can ride for less than the cost of living back home. Jeremy Kroeker (oscillatorpress.com) has gone riding for months in places like Turkey and Syria. He has done it cost effectively, had a great adventure, and come home with no major costs. Don't believe me: read his books. A student I trained, Phil (r-atw.com), has been riding all over South America. At the time I wrote this, he was on day 449. He works remotely to cover the costs and since travel costs are cheap down in South America, I don't see him ever coming "home." The limits of where you can ride your motorcycle are up to you and your wallet. For rides that require shipping over land, the price point is usually less than the cost of hotels, food, and wear and tear. It also saves a lot of time. Shipping your motorcycle will allow you to ride much farther away with less time taken away from work and family. The work to make it happen will be worth the life-changing adventure that awaits you.

The unplanned plan

You can plan your ride as much as you want, but I guarantee things will change. Don't get me wrong, you should still plan out the ride. But the skill of rolling with the changes is a good one.

One ride really tested my ability to roll with the punches started out back home. I was at a track day with my motorcycle. My plan was to have a few fun laps and get the bike shipped to San Francisco (from Vancouver) for the start of my ride. I was four laps into my track day when something snapped on my bike, and it started puking oil. My day was cut short, and my big ride was literally up in smoke. I sent a message to my buddy about the bad news. Being a great riding buddy, he offered up his second motorcycle. I said sure, not wanting to miss out on what would be my only big ride for the season. I flew down with as many of my accessories and things I needed for my trip as possible. I setup my motorcycle as best I could, and away we went. The breakdown initially seemed like a blessing in disguise; my bike could have broken down in the middle of Death Valley. Not so fast, though – the borrowed bike soon started leaking fork oil. We did our best to clean out the seal, but there was no roadside fix. The bike needed a full service. We made it to the Ducati dealer in Las Vegas, which we were very thankful for. The bike needed to be there for two days. Now what? We could easily have stayed in Vegas for two extra days, but on a motorcycle trip you crave big, open, quiet spaces. We checked out rental options for motorcycles and cars. Renting an SUV seemed like the best option. With a little luck (really?), we ended up with a substantial upgrade and drove a brand-new Cadillac Escalade for two days. We drove through Zion National Park, Horseshoe Bend, and Monument Valley. This was serious mileage that would have been too long and uncomfortable on a motorcycle. We even avoided a good rain storm riding in the covered comfort of Cadillac luxury. But although it was only two days, we were itching to get riding again. Getting back onto the motorcycles was more exciting that it should have been. That's how perseverance feels. We had another three days of riding back through Death Valley, the Sequoias, Yosemite, and Stanislaus. In the end, our motorcycle ride turned out to be better than planned. I would never plan to rent a car on a motorcycle ride because that is ridiculous. Good luck selling that to your buddies. I could have easily given up on this ride, and most people would have. But then I would have missed out on a great ride and would have settled on a very quiet riding season. Looking back, I would not change a thing about this ride.

Big group rides are what propelled my love of motorcycle riding, so don't ignore this. Give it a try. The friendships and relationships you forge could very well be the ones you have for the rest of your life. In the world we live in, we are constantly connected to everything. Riding a motorcycle requires focus, and it can be meditative. Add in riding in faraway places, and you get the true reset and relaxation.

Chapter FOURTEEN

Track Days

Most riders don't make it to a track day. That's a mistake, so do not skip this chapter. Track days are for every motorcyclist. This is where you get to expand your abilities as a rider and find the limits of your motorcycle. Driving a car, you can get away with inexperience. On a motorcycle, it is essential to learn to a higher degree to reduce your risk of crashing on the street. Yes, you will face an increased chance of crashing your motorcycle, but you will decrease your chance of crashing on the street. This is an excellent tradeoff. A track is a much safer place to expand your skills. This could be a small track setup in an empty parking lot or a full-sized race track open to the public. Grab your favorite riding buddies and grow your motorcycle skills together.

What you need

All you need to participate in a track day is you, your motorcycle, and full motorcycle gear. This does not mean you need full motorcycle racing leathers. As long as you are wearing full gear and a full-face helmet, you can join a track day. It is a common misconception that there is a long list of requirements to join a track. If you are really fast on your motorcycle and you want to join the faster groups, then you will need top-notch gear.

All motorcycles are welcome on the track. This includes dirt bikes, cruisers, touring bikes, and scramblers. If it has two wheels, bring it. You'll see mostly sport bikes, but you'll be placed in a group that is safe for you. Your motorcycle may need nothing added or taken away from it. Some track days require you to tape up your lights and reflectors (using painter's tape). There are a few reasons for this. One is distractions. A bright light may distract a rider and break their concentration. Second, the glass or plastic coverings can shatter, making a mess of the track. Taping them up reduces the cleanup. That is really it. Your prep will, at most, require a roll of painter's tape.

Additional and recommended requirements for your motorcycle are a full tank of gas and even a jerry can in case you run out. Removing your mirrors is a good idea: you are only concerned about what is ahead of you and organizers do not want you to be using your mirrors. You won't need your headlights either, so you can remove the fuses from your fuse box. This prevents them from turning on. If they do not light up, you may not need to tape them up.

How does it work?

Safety is the primary concern at track days. It is not a free-for-all out on the track. They will group you according to your skill level and motorcycle. If this is your first track day, you will be in the beginner group. This does not mean you are a beginner motorcyclist: it means you are a beginner at the track. It is up to you to prove to the track riders and staff that you have the skills to move to a larger group. Do not make this decision on your own.

The riders meeting at the start of the day is for everyone. These are the rules for the track. Everyone needs to be on the same page, knowing what is acceptable and not acceptable. Each rider group has different rules. The beginner group will allow passing on the straight sections but not in corners. The more advanced groups will have more liberal passing rules. There will also be several flags waved on the track. These are used to communicate very important information such as a warning in a corner, a crash, or when it's time to get off the track. They will not let you out on the track if you do not participate in the riders meeting. Track days are made much safer having these rules and meetings in place.

Your motorcycle will have to be inspected for safety before you are allowed to enter the track. It is a thorough check to see that nothing is leaking from your motorcycle, that nothing will fall off, and that your motorcycle is in good working order. If everything checks out, you will get an approval sticker; if not, then you will have to get the problem fixed. If you have a problem, there are plenty of people to help you out. This is where you want to find the problems and not when you're riding at 200 km/h (124 mph).

It's go time!

So how much track time do you get? It varies, but you will be exhausted by the end of the day. You'll get six to seven sessions lasting fifteen to twenty minutes each. This may not seem like a lot, but this will be the most intense riding you will ever do. Your session will probably not be the first of the day, so this will give you time to talk to the instructors about the track. Before you know it, you'll be getting ready and heading out to the pit lane for launch.

Now it is definitely go time. You'll be lined up with everyone, waiting. Anxiety and expectations will be high. They'll point at you and off you go. They let you out in smaller groups with a leader. The leader will show you the lines of the track, which are the best lines to take to get through the track smoothly. It will take time to learn the track, so do not get upset with yourself. After your first session, there is a high chance you'll feel overwhelmed. You'll also feel like you have a long way to go. All normal. Your second session will start off the same, but you will start to develop flow. Flow is that smoothness that comes with riding. You're learning the track and finding the good lines. It is still good to use the safety riders and coaches; following them will accelerate your learning. After this session, you should start to be feeling much better about your day. The third session is when the magic happens. You know the track well enough and you can start pushing yourself outside your comfort zone. This is where you'll see the great value of a track day. This is where you become the better, faster rider. This may also be your new addiction.

After three sessions, it is lunch time. Time to refuel and rest up for the rest of the day. You'll have three to four more sessions. It is key not to eat a big lunch. I rarely see healthy meals at track days. Since you're already fatiguing both physically and mentally, you're likely to make a poor choice. Bring your own lunch, a healthy lunch. Nothing loaded with carbs. Stick to a good lunch of protein, natural fats, and carbs, but not too many carbs. When I see a rider eat a burger and fries (or something similar) for a lunch, I usually also see them later in the afternoon almost out of energy from the food coma they have induced. You'll need to keep your mind fast and focused. That is impossible with a heavy lunch. The afternoon sessions can be your fastest but only if you plan them.

Once you're up for your fourth session, you'll be quick to get back into the groove. You may even start to pass other riders. Be respectful about this. This and your future sessions will be good ones to work on your body positioning. Everything will really come together. You're finally riding your motorcycle to its full capabilities. You'll have a good understanding of what it is capable of. Best of all you'll know what you are capable of. Since this is your first track day, your fatigue may happen sooner than you think. Do not feel you have to complete every session of the day. The best sessions to skip are usually the last. You're tired and you are at a higher risk of making a mistake. This has been a great day, and you're a better rider now. End it on a high note. Leave the track with your new skills, but do not overvalue the experience and training. Use your new skills for good and not evil.

Is it dangerous? Won't I crash?

The tradeoff of the increased risk of your track day is worth the decreased risk on the street. On the track there are no other cars, intersections, people, poles, etc. Every time we ride, we face the risk of crashing. If you know your motorcycle and your skill level for every ride, you will reduce the risk of crashing. If you do happen to crash on the track, congratulations, you just crashed in the safest possible place.

My first crash was at a track day. It was the end of the day, and I was pushing it. I've never leaned my motorcycle over so far. It was exhilarating. Until I watched my motorcycle slide out from under me and I started to slide with it. I slid for what seemed like an impossibly long time. I sat there letting the moment sink in. My bike looked quite sad lying there. I then stood up slowly and wasn't hurt at all. My pride was hurt, and my motorcycle gear scuffed up. My crash was minor and so are most of the crashes that happen on the track. It is rare for an ambulance to take away a rider. Usually when that happens, the rider was attempting something well outside their skill level. You make the choice on how fast you go and how much you want to push your limits.

If you do crash, appreciate the situation. You're learning in a safe environment. Your motorcycle might have a few scuffs or scratches. Nothing a few new parts can't fix. We never want to crash our motorcycles, but it is a requirement to riding motorcycles. It won't happen often and most of the time it is minor (both on and off track). Please don't let the risk of a crash prevent you from going to a track day.

How to get the most out of your track day

This starts with the day before your track day. No late parties or all-night marathons. If you can, have a healthy food day, too. Ensure you will be your best in the morning. You can also use this day to get everything ready. Track days start early, so the less you have to do in the morning, the better. Less to forget, too. When you wake up the next day, all you need to do is roll out of bed and onto your motorcycle (or into your vehicle). Have a good breakfast (more protein, less carbs) and skip the coffee if you can. A track day can bring a lot of anxiety. This is normal, and you will be pushing yourself in a new environment. Coffee makes anxiety worse. Have it after your first or second session.

The riders meeting is mandatory for all, so listen to everything. It will be ten to fifteen minutes of safety information. It will also explain how you can get instruction and the most out of the safety riders. These are your buddies for the day if you choose to use them. I've been a safety rider, and I always have extra time for riders. Most riders at the track just want to ride without instruction. This means extra time for you. If you would like your own instructor, please ask. Some track days do have instructors ready to teach you. You will get the most out of your track day.

There is always a photographer present. They will capture you at your best. This is also a good learning tool as you can see what your body and the motorcycle are doing. You may think you are leaning over, almost to the ground. The pictures tell the whole story. You can buy individual pictures for $10 to $20 or the whole set for $50. Prices vary, but they are worth it. They are professional and perfect for your Instagram account or your wall.

You are allowed to mount your GoPro or various other action cameras. Play around with multiple points on your motorcycle. You can mount your GoPro to your helmet for a great perspective, but it does add weight and wind drag to your helmet. It can also be a safety issue. This is another good learning tool to watch after your track day. You'll be wondering why you keep blowing all the turns. Like the photographs, the videos tell the whole story.

So what is holding you back?

If you get a speeding ticket or any sort of traffic ticket related to speeding, this can easily cost the same as a track day. Maybe even more. The track is where we can satisfy our need for speed, increase our skills, learn our motorcycles, and make a lot of new rider friends. The cost of any track day is pennies on the dollar against crashing or major traffic offenses. The best riders I know (and will ride with) have multiple track-day experiences. They're also the safest riders I know. I can appreciate the anxiety or disinterest in going. I was that person. When I went for the first time, it clicked. This is what makes great riders, it is really what separates the good from the great riders. There are many great riders without track experience, but unless you have a natural talent, it is where you are going to have to go to be the safest rider you want to be. You made the decision to learn to ride, and here you are now loving it. The decision to go to a track day is easier. You already know how to ride; you just want to be safer and better. Get out there and enjoy your motorcycles to their fullest potential.

Chapter FIFTEEN

Racing

If your goal of riding is to race or your first track day was enough to make you want to race, then you need one thing to start: money. If you're going to compete, you are going to have to follow a lot of rules and have a motorcycle eligible for racing. Costs can quickly get out of control. There's also increased risk of crashing. To win races, you will have to ride to 105 per cent of your ability, and that comes with crashes. If you're still with me, then let's get into the details of what will be required.

Let's do this

Get yourself registered for a race course. This will be required for your racing license. They will not let you race without it. They will teach you the techniques, safety, and etiquette. The course is great for your skills, so even if you do not race, you will be a better rider for it. In most of the race courses I have seen, registration is priced very well. They want riders to participate, so don't expect a huge cost yet unless you go for a big-name school.

Obviously, you need a motorcycle, and it will have to be race-ready. This means it can't have lights and it has to be safety-wired. Safety-wired means that anything that can detach from the bike has been tied down with metal wire. I'd recommend that you buy a used race bike to start. Starting with a new motorcycle and prepping it to race can be big money. There are plenty of great used race bikes out there.

Do not spare any expense on your safety gear. You do not need the biggest brand names, but find the best stuff for the best price. Buying used motorcycle gear (not helmets) is fine as long as it is the high-end stuff. You'll need a full-face helmet, leather jacket and pants (one piece recommended), gauntlet gloves, racing boots, and a back protector. Other recommendations are an airbag vest or suit and moisture-wicking clothing to wear underneath.

Now comes the racing membership and the fees associated with it. These won't break your bank, but they are an added cost. The membership fees and racing dues are everything needed to give you the track time you need. Consider getting involved in the race committee if you really get into the racing community. Just like the motorcycle community, the racing community is close—even closer because it is smaller. Everyone helps everyone else out, except on race day. Then you are all sworn enemies fighting for first place.

Choosing a class and motorcycle

Once you take the motorcycle racing course, you'll soon learn you have plenty of classes to race in. You'll start in the novice class, and from there you will be able to choose a direction. The novice class is designed to get you going and learning how to race. After a season racing as a novice, you may have the option to move into a new class or you might need another year as a novice. The class you choose to race in will dictate the motorcycle you buy.

Everyone starts in the small class. The 300 cc (or similar) is where you should seriously consider starting. Not only will this be the easiest way into racing, it will be cost effective as well. The bigger the motorcycle, the more tires and parts you'll need to replace. Big bikes require much more in tires and maintenance because the power they deliver can shred tires fast. The 300-cc class will give much more life on your tires and other consumables such as brakes. Crashing a smaller motorcycle is also a lot cheaper, and crashing is part of racing. Smaller bikes are not as heavy and there is less chance of ending up with a write-off. The bigger they are, the harder they fall.

Once you have the motorcycle and your class figured out, it is time to get sorted with your pit setup. You will soon realize that riding your race bike to your race is not an option (it has no signals and lights), so you will need a truck or trailer. If you are not sure what is best, ask the racing community and see what setups they have. There are various pros and cons to several types of setups. If you already have a vehicle, see what it can tow. If you do not have something suitable for that, it's time to go shopping. Consider buying a van capable of storing a motorcycle because it is much easier to load. Some big trucks make it very difficult to load. Trailers are very low to the ground as well, but then you have to tow a trailer around. In addition to your motorcycle and transportation, you are going to want a tent, chairs, a cooler, tools, and gas. You may even need a generator for your tire warmers if you go this far.

Now you're a racer and where is your sponsorship

You'll quickly hear racers say that if you want to make a million dollars racing, start with three million dollars. Sponsorship certainly helps with the costs, but very few actually get everything paid for and even fewer make a career out of it. This is reserved for the highest level of racing like MotoGP and WSBK. You'll have a much better chance gaining sponsorship by asking for specific things like brakes, helmets, gloves, tires, etc. Money is tight in the motorcycle industry, but there is some to go around. So ask nicely, be a likeable rider, and show you can represent the product. It is very hard to get any level of sponsorship and incredibly easy to lose it. Be an ambassador.

So how about all that money you are going to make? There is definitely some cash for winning races, but considering what's required to win those races, it's hard to keep yourself in the green. You'll need lots of training, the will to risk it in every corner, some luck, and perseverance. Where you will get the biggest reward is the thrill. The biggest reward may very well be the battles you have with the other riders. You and another rider (or more) are battling for sixth place. You pass each other multiple times, you both prey upon each other's weaknesses, but there is no clear winner. Every lap you do, it seems even closer. Who will make the first mistake, who will push themselves even harder? It's unknown but you'll find out soon. If you end up beating out your opponent by milliseconds it will feel better than a first-place finish. This is why so many racers come back every year. Sure, they make no money, but they are pushing themselves personally, mentally, and physically every race. You just can't do this on the street. If you do, your life is likely to be a short one.

Take it to the next level

So what does make a great racer? Great racers are competitive, well-trained, and hard-working. Most of us do not have the natural talent that just makes us go fast. It can be incredibly frustrating to see a racer who barely preps for a race, shows up, and outrides most. Don't compare yourself to them. Focus on yourself. If you're a better racer than you were last race, then you are on the right track. When I look at the top racers of any type of racing, one thing is consistent and that is dirt riding. Being able to ride a dirt bike fast through some sort of course is key to street racing. Enroll yourself in dirt lessons of all types—motocross, flat track, and even enduro. The better your dirt skills are, the better your street skills will be. Go get dirty and make the biggest gains in your speed.

Being fit does play a roll. While I see plenty of riders in poor physical fitness ride incredibly fast, you still need endurance. You won't need to run marathons, but do your stretches, lift heavy things, and have enough cardio to last forty minutes (the length of a typical road race). The key here is consistency: you'll be using specific muscles to race, but you must exercise everything to balance it out. Some muscle groups will not get worked unless you get to the gym. And you can still throw most of this advice out the window if you refuse to eat properly. Nutrition is the defining factor in keeping you healthy. No amount of exercise will work off the effects of excessive burgers, fries, and desserts. No, having a Diet Coke doesn't make it OK either. If you want to ride your motorcycle to first place, the requirements are the same as for an athlete. Train and act like one.

This chapter is just a glimpse of what racing will be. It'll be up to you to determine how involved you're going to be. It is a club filled with the top riders in the world, the best of the best. A mediocre racer can easily be in the top 1 per cent of riders in the world. You'll possess skills 99 per cent of riders are too afraid to learn.

Chapter SIXTEEN

Stunting

A motorcycle pulling a wheelie catches almost everyone's attention. They'll be in awe, they'll be impressed, or they'll be terrified you'll crash into them. It'll carry a thrill and excitement reserved for the biggest adrenaline junkies. It will also come with a painful learning curve for your body. There is good reason that so few people can successfully stunt their motorcycle. One question I am often asked when training is how to wheelie. It's easy enough to learn how to ride on two wheels, but if you want to try to ride with just one, the chasm of difficulty is the size of the Grand Canyon. I couldn't resist the allure of motorcycle wheelies either, and I proceeded to learn on my 600cc Honda F4i. I found the local stunt culture and practiced with them on a quiet industrial road. It was impressive to watch, and I certainly wanted to be like them. When I gathered the courage to try it myself, it was tough. The front wheel would not come up. Then once in a while it would, and it would feel unexpected but thrilling. It's hard to stay concentrated once your risk of getting hurt goes up with that front wheel. But you need this concentration to balance your motorcycle (and you) on one wheel. The front tire will either come back to the ground, or you'll fall off. If you fall off, it will be dramatic. If I still have your attention, read on to see what it takes.

Where are all the stunting schools?

Everything fun in life needs a waiver. Not even Mark Geragos could write the waiver required to attend stunt school. The risk is all on you, so if you decide to learn, you have no one to blame but yourself. Learning to stunt is still an underground business, so bring cash. There are stunters willing to teach you, but you'll have to find them first. Introduce yourself and don't worry about their attitudes. Most of them are shy or feel they need to show bravado. If you're serious, they'll tell you where they practice. Start with buying a used stunt bike. These will be set up already and ready to go. You'll be crashing it, so don't go in thinking this is going to be pretty. Making your own stunt bike costs a lot of money; buying used does not. Once you have the bike, consider getting a truck. Your stunt motorcycle is not geared to ride on the road, so it will be an awful ride. Plus, if you crash it, you'll have a ride home with a truck. Wearing full gear and good gear will lessen the injuries, so don't skimp here. Stunting is a very serious, high-risk activity to get into. It makes motorcycling look like knitting. The biggest injuries you are likely to face are to your wrists and ankles.

Isn't it illegal?

No. Stunting is not illegal. If you find a private parking lot, you can stunt your bike as long as you have permission to be there. It is illegal on the street. Stunting on public roads will get you all sorts of traffic fines and impounds. If you are using private property to stunt, be respectful. You can be kicked off at any time. It is much harder to be kicked off if you are being kind. You may also be doing the owners a favor by being there watching things. The authorities also appreciate you stunting off public roads. If you show everyone good behavior, expect to be treated better as well. They may even want to watch. Stunting is easily vilified, and if you ask most people, they assume it is illegal. It is hard enough to learn, so don't make it harder by learning in the wrong places.

Yeah, yeah, yeah... So how do I wheelie my motorcycle?!

This is a quick explanation of what I have tried and what has been recommended to me. Don't take this explanation as the exact way to do it. A few words in a book is no replacement for a stunt instructor and your practice time. Make sure you visit YouTube to see all the different ways things can go wrong with stunting. Almost any motorcycle can wheelie. So if you are going to try this on your own, find a nice quiet space and bring a buddy for safety. Rev the motorcycle up and get rolling. Slower speed is good; higher speed means bigger risk. Pull the clutch in, rev it up more, and let the clutch out. If you don't have enough power, the bike will accelerate. If you have just the right amount, the front end will come up. If you have too much throttle, the front end will come up so fast that you'll loop the bike right over on top of yourself. This is why you have to be very good with your rear brake. The rear brake brings the front end down if it gets too high, but it is sensitive, so too much and you'll slam your front end to the ground. The moment the front tire leaves the ground, it'll feel as if your bike is standing straight up in the air; in reality, the wheel is probably just off the ground. You'll need to be able to control the clutch, throttle, and rear brake all at the same time while the front wheel climbs into the air. If you practice this enough and survive the falls, you'll find your balance point. This is the magical point where the motorcycle is stable on one wheel. It is different for every motorcycle.

When I ask riders how they can wheelie every motorcycle they ride, it usually comes down to lots of practice they got when they were younger riding dirt bikes. Riding dirt bikes to learn how to wheelie is a common answer. Since they were younger, it was easier to survive the fall unhurt. By now, I hope you are coming to the realization that falling off your motorcycle while learning any sort of stunting is going to happen often. I don't recommend it, as some injuries can take you out for weeks. If you have family obligations, work obligations, or just like living without injuries, stunting may not be for you. If you just can't ignore the urge, try a unicycle. It is essentially what you are doing on a motorcycle — riding on one wheel. A unicycle will start to show you what sort of balance is required. Good luck?

Chapter SEVENTEEN

Advanced Rider Training

The key to your long-term safety on a motorcycle is ongoing education and training. Not only will you have better odds of coming home safely, but you'll have a proficiency level equal to professional athletes, dancers, and even American Ninja Warriors. With this level of understanding and skill, the enjoyment you get from riding will skyrocket. These are bold statements, but I assure you they are not exaggerations. Taking any form of advanced rider training enhances your skill on your own motorcycle and on any others as well. Most riders never take any form of advanced rider training. Someone who applies and gets hired to work at McDonald's will get more training than the average motorcyclist. Think about that for a moment. I will shout from rooftops, on social media, and at my students, but the attendance is still quite low. It can be scary pushing yourself on your motorcycle. You don't want to damage your motorcycle or worse, Injure yourself. It's understandable, but the benefits you'll receive are worth the risk a hundred times over. Don't wait around to take advanced courses; take them as often as your schedule and budget allows. Consider them pennies on the dollar on how much a crash can cost you.

Whichever motorcycle you currently own, take a course that uses that motorcycle. Most likely, you'll have to use yours, but they may include a motorcycle for your use. Let's say you own a mid-sized cruiser—taking a slow-speed maneuvering course is a great start. Make the decision easy and take the first advanced course you can. All kinds of advanced riding courses benefit the rider. The best motorcycle riders I know (the ones who win races) have dirt-riding skills. In my opinion, dirt riding should be a requirement for street riding. Round out your experience and take different courses. Even riding a bicycle can benefit your motorcycle-riding skills. It is still two wheels.

The first easy step to advanced rider training could be reading a book, listening to a podcast, or watching YouTube videos. There are not too many books out there, so you shouldn't feel overwhelmed. Not much of a reader? Buy the audiobooks. Here is a list of the big ones out there, in no particular order:

Total Control: High Performance Street Riding Techniques by Lee Parks

Proficient Motorcycling: The Ultimate Guide to Riding Well by David L. Hough

Mastering the Ride: More Proficient Motorcycling by David L. Hough

A Twist of the Wrist, Volumes I & II by Keith Code

Sport-Riding Techniques by Nick Ienatsch

Motorcycle Roadcraft: The Police Rider's Handbook Smooth Riding

The Pridmore Way by Reg Pridmore

Adventure Riding Techniques: The Essential Guide to All the Skills You Need for Off-Road Adventure Riding by Robert Wicks and Greg Baker

Podcasts are great and free. They're an excellent way to make your driving time more enjoyable. In no particular order, check these ones out:

Ken Hill Coaching
Adventure Rider Radio
Two Enthusiasts
Motorcycles & Misfits
False Neutral Podcast
Front End Chatter
Loud Pipes!

YouTube continues to be a great way to educate yourself on almost anything. If you can't ride because of the weather or winter season, why not watch some videos? There are plenty of videos to watch, and all of them are free. They'll give you ideas and "ah ha!" moments on how to learn on your machine. Just please be careful. Watching a video and then trying new skills on public roads is risky. Find an empty parking lot and always practice with a buddy.

These are the most cost-effective ways to become a better, safer rider. They're an excellent supplement to the real thing of learning in a course. You should be willing to open up your wallet and take an advanced rider course. The costs range from $100 to $2,000 or more. As mentioned, they will be worth it, but until you take a course you won't know.

Remember that the good riders, the safe riders, and the riders having the most fun, take these courses.

Push yourself to grow yourself

With all the options you have, you'll want to know what you should do first. If a student asks me what they should do next after learning to ride, I give them three options. Take a slow-speed maneuvering course, a Gymkhana cone course (small track day), or a dirt-riding course. These three courses offer the essential tripod of skills and put you at the top. This makes you an above-average rider quickly. Given that so few riders take advanced courses, it is not hard to become better than everyone else.

The slow-speed maneuvering course can also be closely related to a ride-like-a-cop course. The motorcycles that cops use are big and cumbersome, and they don't look capable. Never think you can outrun a cop on a motorcycle. These are highly trained riders, and they get to take courses regular civilians are not allowed to take. Thankfully, some enterprising retired cops have started up these programs all over the place. You should be able to find one in most major cities. Most of these courses will get you to use your own motorcycle, which is the proper way. Every rider should really learn how to ride their own machine. Even if the course does provide the motorcycles, you still get huge benefits. You may even push yourself a little harder because it is not your ride. From the courses I have taken and taught, I can say it really comes down to clutch control. Most riders do not use it enough. This course forces you to. With some verbal teaching then practicing, you'll be able to maneuver your motorcycle through tight figure eights. This will grow into tight turns from stopping, emergency stopping with a swerve to avoid, and even a timed course you must ride through. At the end of this course, it will be impressive what you can do with your motorcycle. I have great memories of my time at the Northwest Motorcycle School. I ride mostly sport bikes, so getting on an older Kawasaki Kz1000 (the bike from *CHiPs*) seemed very unnatural. Operating this heavy cruiser at impossibly low speeds was tough. I had to fall off it several times because I was learning. The falls were at low speeds, so it was only my ego that took a light bruising. As the course progressed, so did the challenges and the track. The whole thing finished with a timed lap around the entire course. When it was my time to go, I was under the pressure of a stopwatch, my spectating colleagues, and several hundred orange cones in tight quarters. It was intense and a thrill. It is what I imagine athletes have to go through during an Olympic medal round. In the end, I did great and this sport-bike rider had an incredible amount of fun to go along with some new skills.

Dirt riding is accessible almost anywhere, so these facilities are a short search away. Riding in limited traction is an incredible skill to have. On the street we get traction most of the time. A motorcycle will be just fine if it slips a little here and there. It is not a big deal. If the rider is not ready for it, the rider can overreact. Overreacting causes crashes. Dirt riding teaches us to relax and let the motorcycle sort itself out. A motorcycle does not like panic braking or cutting the throttle off. Most likely, everything will be OK as long as we maintain what we were doing beforehand. This takes training, understanding, and trust. I started riding on the street, and I stayed on the street for years. When I finally ventured into dirt riding, I realized how much I was missing out on, not just in the fun of dirt riding, but also in the important skills it teaches. So I took courses, and the course that changed my riding for the better was American Supercamp. This program runs all over the United States and is well worth the trip to attend it. It is also one of the best deals because they provide the motorcycles and gear. The two-day program starts you off with the basics and you expand your skills throughout the entire course. It starts with an oval course, then at the end you have a full course with all sort of turns. Best of all, it has the most qualified instructors—championship racers, for example. It's a thrilling two days and at the end you want more. That is why people commonly come back for repeat courses, me included. Dirt riding teaches you skills that just cannot be learned on the street. If you love it, you can expand it into Motocross which is dirt bikes with jumps. There is also flat-track riding, which involves an oval course in which you consistently slide the back end of your motorcycle around turns. It's similar to drifting a car. It really is a whole new world of skills and riding.

Higher speeds are common and easy to achieve on most motorcycles. Given that our speed limits really do limit out motorcycles, taking it to the track is the safest and most fun way to see what your motorcycle can do. When we put ourselves in a learning environment, we are much more receptive to pushing our limits. The track can be intimidating, but only if you allow it to be. At all track days there will be support staff to ensure you have a safe and fun day. Tracks vary in size, too. It could be a Gymkhana course (lots of orange cones) or a full-sized, professional race course.

Racing can be similar to track days, but there is some racing etiquette that is incredibly important. If you want to see what racing is all about, take the race license course. Even if you don't want to race, the education is worth it. That was my approach when I brought my sport-touring motorcycle, a Honda VFR, to the race course. Learning all about racing makes it more fun to watch. Launch control (think drag race) is a thrill, and, of course, cornering and braking are key. Given the amount of track time you get these can be great deals.

I haven't seen very many courses offering adventure (enduro) motorcycles to learn on, so you'll most likely have to bring your own. If you're too afraid of potentially dropping your adventure motorcycle during a course, then you really shouldn't be riding one. They're designed for falling, so all you'll have to do is pick it up. It might get a few scratches and dings, but those are badges of honour. Dirt bikes and adventure bikes do share the same set of rules, but the big difference is weight. Your adventure bike will be heavier. You'll have to manage that weight while being in a constant state of limited traction. It sounds scarier than it actually is— just keep the throttle on to keep control. Your rear brake will be your friend, and your front brake will be used sparingly. It'll be easy to be intimidated by dirt roads (especially downhill ones) so the right training makes this a simple one. Even on the pavement you'll be dealing with road construction, which will consist of similar limited traction. So even if you're a pavement princess, these dirt skills still come in handy. I remember a road I was riding down in southern California. A major storm from a leftover hurricane had passed through a few days before. As I descended down this beautiful, twisty road it soon turned light brown from all the run off. The road was fully covered with light brown silt and dirt. This does not feel great on any motorcycle. You have to be very careful with the brakes, even though the motorcycle wants to speed up since you're going downhill and you have tight corners to navigate through. You'll be tense when you should relax, and you'll have to trust the motorcycle to stay upright (this is hard to do). Your adventure bike will take on everything you want it to, even crossing rivers. I hope you are ready for it.

California SuperBike School is one of the oldest and coolest courses still around. It was started by Keith Code in 1976. It has evolved into four levels of courses, and it includes the slide bike. The slide bike shows you just how much you can lean a bike over before you crash. This would be the course that costs $2,000+ for all four days, but they do provide motorcycles if you need one. Not just any motorcycles, either: at the time of this writing, they use BMW S1000RRs. This program is top level all the way through. If you are lucky enough to attend one of the many courses around the world, you'll feel like royalty. To find out if a California SuperBike School is near you or if they are coming to a track near you, best visit their website and contact them. Even if you don't ride sport bikes, the experience alone would be a lifetime memory.

Are you still reading? Good!

I hope this chapter gets you excited about taking your riding to the next level. Don't be afraid to jump in and go for it. The longer you wait, the more bad habits creep in. Take these courses while you are still new, if you're rusty, or if you just want to evolve your riding. It is very rare to talk to someone who did not have a good experience at an advanced rider training course. Most feel like they now possess superhero riding skills after just one course. Imagine how you'll feel after a few courses. There is a word of caution with this training: do not over value it. It is easy to get overconfident on a motorcycle. Just because you took an advanced rider training course doesn't mean you're a professional.

Personally, I take at least one advanced course per year. It keeps the rust off my skills, and it is a highlight of my motorcycling season. If more and more riders take advanced courses, the stats for riders will get better and better. Have fun.

Chapter EIGHTEEN

Motorcycle Theft Prevention

Since the love of your motorcycle can easily exceed your car. How would you feel if someone stole it? Let's not even go there. Prevention is absolutely key to never losing your motorcycle. Do not get complacent with your motorcycles security. Now that said, I have parked my motorcycle all over the western United States and Baja Mexico without locks and it was still there in the morning. However, one morning when

I woke up and went to work it was not there. It has been the only motorcycle that has been stolen from me and the feeling is awful. I saw the empty space where it was and I thought I parked it elsewhere. It took me a good ten minutes for me to accept the fact that my ride was gone. The ride that I rode everywhere on. I had great memories with my Kawasaki Ninja 1000. Now what? I called the police, filed a report. I called my insurance company and let them know the bad news. I was hoping my motorcycle would be quickly recovered but to this day it has not. I was hopeful as 40% of motorcycles are recovered but sometimes you may not want it back. So what can you do?

Where your motorcycle is parked is important. If it is consistently in the same place, that is the most likely place it will get stolen. First step in prevention is to cover it. Out of sight. Out of mind. If your motorcycle attracts attention, it might attract the wrong attention. Keep it covered with a motorcycle specific cover so it is just a grey blob in the background. Thieves may be snooping so they will still find your motorcycle. If and when they do they would much rather ride your motorcycle away then load it into a truck or van. It is much easier to get away from you or the cops if the thief can speed away on your motorcycle.

Always lock it up

Thieves are typically lazy so lock it up. Start with your steering column lock. Place your key in your motorcycle ignition, turn the handle bars all the way to the left, now take your key and turn it all the way left to the lock position and remove the key. Now the handlebars are locked. This is good but merely a simple annoyance for the thief. This is where locks come in. Not just one lock either. Use two or more. This is more work than the thief may want to do. It does mean you have extra steps when parking and going for a ride. I promise you it will be worth it so you do not have to deal with the anguish of losing your ride. So how many options do you have?

Let's start with chains and locks. The heavier duty the better. They will be used through your motorcycle wheels, the back tire preferably. It is harder to remove the back tire versus the front tire. Motorcycle dealers and bicycle shops have some of the best chains money can buy. They are limited by the lock you use. If you spend good money on a great chain do not buy a $20 lock. Which lock is best? A lock that is heavy in your hand and the shackle is mostly covered. A Master Pro Series 6321 is worth your consideration. Cost for this setup will be between $100 and $200. I would also highly recommend visiting YouTube and searching out videos by the Lock Picking Lawyer. Great information on locks but disappointing how easily most locks can be defeated.

You can also anchor the motorcycle to the ground. This may require professional installation as a concrete anchor requires heavy duty tools to implement. Having a metal ring in the concrete (or similar) means your motorcycle can't be taken away. Just locking it is good but if the thieves bring a wheelbarrow or a cart, they can take it away and deal with the locks later. There are kits available that can be anchored into the ground. This is an excellent defense.

Disc locks and brake lever locks prevent the motorcycle from being moved. A brake lever lock will squeeze the front brake lever and prevent it from being rolled away. It is a neat design but relatively new to the security options of your motorcycle. The disc lock is usually highly visible and comes with the bright orange elastic cable. This bright orange cable attaches to your handlebar as a reminder to take your disc lock off before riding away. These locks are designed to slide onto the brake rotor. The disc lock uses the holes or spaces in the rotor. This is an excellent design the shackle is covered by the lock housing. It can be difficult to defeat unless the shackle is thin. It which case a hammer could break it. What I like about disc locks is there size. They are easy enough to be carried around with you while you ride. So wherever you go, you can take it with you.

Alarms are an option as no thief wants to attract attention. If the horn of the alarm is exposed the thief could disable it quickly. You should also consider how much you pay attention to alarms yourself. Most people don't even hear alarms anymore. It just becomes part of the background noise of a city. Alarms also are an extra drain on your battery. If you leave your motorcycle longer than ten days, your alarm may have drained the battery. I am not a big fan of alarms for these reasons.

Tracking it is possible if you're willing to pay the price for it. You will have to buy the tracking unit and pay the monthly fee for it. As long as the thief doesn't find it or know, you should be able to find your motorcycle. That said, be careful tracking it down yourself. You do not know who you are dealing with. It is tricky reporting it to the police. They can't just kick in doors, shoot first, ask questions later if you tell them where your motorcycle is. They have a process they must follow and property rights must be followed.

How I steal motorcycles

One day I had to steal a motorcycle. Yes, you read that right. I had a student of mine call me and ask for help. His motorcycle was broken down and he was nowhere near it. By luck, I was. I was driving in the company van so I had room to move a motorcycle. I went down and check it out myself. It was located in a parking lot downtown. I found it and luckily the steering lock was not engaged. I proceeded to push the motorcycle out of the parking lot. When I got to the parking attendant they asked for my parking ticket. Of course I did not have it and asked about the minimum cost. It required a form and by this time there was a line of cars behind be getting impatient. Once the parking lot attendant become impatient, he just let me go. Here I am in my plain street clothes, no motorcycle gear, pushing a motorcycle out of a 'secure' parking lot. I continued to push the motorcycle down the sidewalk, into the alley and into my waiting van. I was surprised as you are right now. Take this as a lesson to lock your motorcycle up, every single time. I might be out there!

You may feel anxiety when parking your motorcycle. This is normal but do exercise some degree of security. Thieves are typically lazy and go for the low hanging fruit. A small amount of prevention can make a big difference. If you have something nicer and it consistently parked in a well lit, quiet place. You will have to go the extra mile to lock it up. If you park your motorcycle in an underground parking lot. Check to see what the other motorcyclists are doing for locks. Make sure you know who they are too. As motorcyclists we need to stick together and watch out for our stuff. That said, see what they are doing for locks and lock it up a little more than they do.

The insurance process

If your motorcycle does get stolen. Call the police and get a report started. You'll need a file number and then you can call your insurance company. There will be a waiting period before they can proceed with paying you out. This is typically thirty days. When they're deciding what your payout amount is, be sure to be informed with replacement costs. Have ads of similar motorcycles for sale ready to show your insurance company. Keep in mind, if there is a loan for the motorcycle the cheque must be sent to the bank first. When the money does arrive, try to look on the bright side and enjoy your new bike day.

Motorcycle theft does not happen that often it just feels like it is a common occurrence. Motorcycles are getting harder and harder steal and with a little effort on your part. You'll never have to worry about losing your ride.

Chapter NINETEEN

Becoming a Motorcycle Instructor

I went from riding a desk to riding motorcycles for a career. Sounds appealing, doesn't it? It is. Several students have told me they want to become an instructor soon after they learn to ride. As of today, some of them are. So yes, teaching people how to ride is as fun as it sounds. Think about it: you get to teach someone a skill that they are really excited to learn. It is work that never really feels like work. Being a motorcycle instructor can be very rewarding personally.

What makes a great motorcycle instructor?

Communication is the single biggest factor to being a good instructor. Of course, there are plenty of other factors, but we'll focus on this one first. You could teach an entire class of students how to ride and all of them might fail. You do speak the same language, but do they understand it? Are you making them feel good and excited? There is a teaching language, and that language is unique to everyone. The way you describe things can make perfect sense to you, but to others it might as well be a foreign language. No one instructor can match their teaching language to all students, but you can get the message across to most. This is why I really like to have two or more instructors on the training lot. It gives a better chance that all students understand what is being taught. You'll absolutely need a lot of feedback on your teaching method regardless, and you need to be open to changing it. You are going to make a lasting impression on your students, so communication is key. Some of the best motorcycle riders in the world couldn't teach clutch control because when they do it, they "just do it." Learn how to explain things in several different ways and use analogies as much as possible. Even better, inject some humour into it. Get excited about it. Education without emotion will not be remembered. I'll always take an enthusiastic instructor with limited motorcycling experience over the professional rider with a monotone voice.

Have you ever been frustrated when explaining something to a friend or family? Now imagine a class full of people making the same mistake over and over after your excellent (or so you thought) instruction. It's hard not to hop on the nearest motorcycle and ride it into oncoming traffic. Your patience has to transform into superhero perseverance and calm. The student will already be losing patience, so you must keep calm explaining it to them for the tenth time. If you show frustration, you'll make the learning environment difficult. Now the student is not having a good time. Patience is a skill. It will take time to develop it and when you do, it will help with several things in life, too.

For most people, learning to ride is a dream come true. It's been on their to-do list for a long time. Be relaxed and be the motorcycle rider they imagine. Smile, be easygoing, and laugh easily. Right from the moment you meet them, you should be professional, but be a person they would want to ride with as well. If they feel comfortable with you, they will learn much better. How a person feels is the strongest factor in how they learn. Communication is key, but the way a student feels is a close second. They are looking to make motorcycling their next big thing. Make them feel the excitement of riding and keep it there while they learn.

Requirements and expectations from you

The requirements for teaching people how to ride are low. In my province (British Columbia, Canada) you need three years with a full motorcycle license, and you need to pass a police background check and a health check from your doctor. These are minimal requirements for teaching a skill. All you would need to do is get your full license, sit around for three years, avoid breaking any laws, and exercise at least a little bit. Then get someone to hire you. You do not need to have motorcycle racing trophies, write numerous articles, or even author books, but those things do help.

Again, communication and enthusiasm are the most important things. However, I did not feel this way coming into the industry. We all have egos, and they can be fragile. Since I did not have race trophies or much else other than the actual riding, I did feel inadequate. Months into my teaching, when my confidence really came through in my posture and words, I realized the real requirements to riding — they're what I've been talking about repeatedly in this book. If you want to teach, don't worry about your missing accolades. Focus on the message you will deliver.

Never tell a student they shouldn't ride motorcycles

It is not up to you to deliver this message. Everyone can ride motorcycles. Whether they really should is up to them. Your job is to teach, communicate, and encourage. You can get them through the course with enough patience and time. At my school, we allow students to come back as much as they want until they pass. They will be discouraged, but they know they can try again. I do recommend they ride a bicycle in the meantime, as this is a big help. I wish all students would ride bicycles before learning to ride. It really helps. When they come back, most will pass. With those that don't, it is going to take some extra time. That is OK. These are the people who probably shouldn't ride. It is extremely important that they fail with you and not out in the real world. The real world has serious consequences and your training lot does not. If the student is truly a two-wheeled disaster, then after enough crashing they will come to the decision themselves. They must come to the decision themselves. If you are the one to deliver the message, expect bad reviews. You're also going to affect their lives as well; no one likes to fail.

This is where your patience is really tested as an instructor. It is also what separates the good instructors from the great. Don't expect to be able to teach everyone how to ride. You must identify the challenged students and rotate instructors. The challenged students need exposure to as many teaching languages as possible. If you succeed, the reward is there. You've shaped that student's life. Don't discount how important this is to any student.

The key to happiness for you and your student

Teaching people a skill just feels good. It is also a period of time where everyone listens to you. They are focused on your words and not their smartphones. You're the first person they trust to teach them to ride. They will remember you.

Months and years after you teach them, they come up to you and remember your name. It is tough to remember all their names, but it's understandable. You will experience a deep level of satisfaction when you see the student's first motorcycle and their smile is so big it can be seen from space.

If this interests you, then your first step is to seek out your favorite motorcycle school and ask to help out. No better way to get your foot in the door than by offering your time. This could be helping out with student road rides, kicking orange cones around, or setting up and cleaning up. Make yourself an asset to the school, and they'll have no choice but to give you a job. It will most likely be a weekend job, as that is when most schools run. It is an excellent way to spend a weekend and definitely better than couch-surfing. If you find enough enjoyment in it, you may even venture into opening up your own school. I certainly do not regret it.

Conclusion

Can you see what a fun and exciting world, riding can be? Embrace it and the people that come along with it. The people you meet could lead to new friends, exciting trips, jobs, opportunities, and even someone you spend the rest of your life with. I am not overselling motorcycling. It really can be everything you want it to be. It is up to you to get involved and be social. Even if you consider yourself an introvert, you'll be amazed the confidence riding motorcycles can give you. In a way we become the people we want to be when we wear the motorcycle gear. It is like our very own super hero suit. You then might find the hardest thing about riding is finding the time. With such busy lives we live, it is harder and harder to disconnect. Your motorcycle forces you to disconnect and enjoy life on your terms. You'll get the full experience of the enjoyment and thrills. It is so hard to quiet our minds (meditating is hard), the motorcycle gives us the calm clarity we need. It is something I see more and more on why people are getting into riding. Can you think of anything else in your life that prevents you from looking at your phone? It does come with increased risk but that is what makes us feel alive. Riding a motorcycle will always put you in the minority of your friends. It is just too scary for most. I am fine with that as it keeps it special for us. It's the reason why we wave to other riders on the road we don't know. It is why riders will help other riders out just based on the fact that you ride motorcycles. The community of riding is alive and well.

You've seen almost everything riding can do for you. You'll also be safer out there knowing what to do and what not to do. Motorcycling will always be constantly evolving and changing along with the way. There will always be something cool to ride and people to ride it with. I wanted to get as much as I know about motorcycling in this book. It is from my personal experiences and what a ride it has been. From the moment I learned to ride to now, it's enhanced my life so much. Which leads me to the most important and impactful story of motorcycling. I wanted to ride from the moment I saw them on the road. I just knew I had to do it. Years went by and I never knew anyone who did. I wasn't adventurous yet so I didn't have the confidence to go at it on my own. That all changed when the girl I was dating had a roommate. Lionel rode motorcycles and his brother ran a motorcycle school. All of a sudden I was enrolled and learning to ride. From that point on I rode my motorcycle as much as I can. The enthusiasm of a new rider allows you to ride In cold or hot weather, heavy traffic, and just about any type of riding. I did stay in touch with Lionel over the years and almost ten years later we decided to open a motorcycle school together. That worked out incredibly well. You never know who you will meet and what it will mean to you. I would be living a different life had I learned to ride earlier or later.

Thank you for supporting my way of life. I hope you have just as much fun (or even more) than I have had riding two wheels. Tell everyone how much fun it is and please tell me. I love riding stories. If you want to follow me along on my adventures. Please visit www.ridefar.ca You can also find me on YouTube and at 1stgear.ca (my school). What would be the biggest compliment would be a review on Amazon or wherever you purchased this book from. The more reviews I have the more people will read it. This will keep me riding and writing. I have bigger projects in mind and I'll need your support to do them. If you ever see me on a ride, track day or where there are two wheels, please say hi. If I see you on the road, I'll wave. Ride FAR and ride safe!

Lee RideFar

ridefar.ca

1stgear.ca

leeridefar@gmail.com

Acknowledgements

To everyone I work with at 1st Gear. We get to work outside, teach people, and have a lot of fun doing it. They call it work but working with you makes it fun. It's been five years since 1st Gear started. It would not be as successful as it is today if it were not for you. I'm incredibly lucky to ride with you and teach with you. Thank you Mel, Adam, Patrick, Carol, Raymond, Nicola, Otto, John, Bruce, and Lionel.

Where would I be without all the students that chose my school? Thank you. Not only have you learned to ride but you make me a better rider too. I always want to ensure that your hard earned money is going to give you a great start in riding motorcycles. It pushes me to go out there, take courses, write, and educate as many people as I can. It's a thrill seeing and riding with the riders I taught.

My editors, Jessica & Raine. Thank you for polishing my words into a professional piece of writing. I barely made it through high school English and over time it did get better but there is no way I would have been able to publish this book without your eyes and expertise. You'll have a great career editing and everything else that comes along with it.

My rider buddies who added their opinions and ideas. I know a lot about riding but I know different sets of eyes see different things. I missed some key things and I was able to include them. Thank you to Adam G, Shane A, Kevin M, Patrick M, Steve P, Lionel G, Don S, Jay T, Sergio G, Matt B, Bruce W, Dean D, John, Darren, Claudia, Tanya, Frank M, and Adam Sky. If I missed someone I didn't mean it!

Australia! You, big beautiful country. You're a legend. This book was started there and all the sunshine, beaches and beauty made it easy for the words to flow from my mind to these pages. I'll be back soon and maybe one day permanently.

About The Author

Lee learned to ride in 2005. Since then motorcycling took over his life and became a way of life. You'll find him riding his motorcycle on big trips and big tracks or backpacking his way around the world. When he is at home, he teaches new riders to ride at 1st Gear Motorcycle Training and pets/chases/plays with his cat, Sprocket. You can also find him at his website, ridefar.ca and YouTube for reviews, opinions, and education.